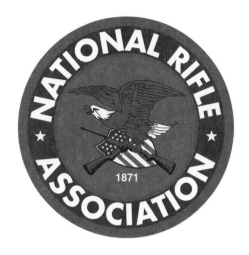

NRAMUSEUM.COM

THE NRA NATIONAL FIREARMS MUSEUM
GUN COLLECTOR'S LOGBOOK

The personal Gun Collection Logbook of: _____

Logbook No._____ Beginning date:_____ Ending date:_____

**CHARTWELL
BOOKS, INC.**

This edition published in 2012 by
CHARTWELL BOOKS, INC.
A division of BOOK SALES, INC.
276 Fifth Avenue, Suite 206
New York, New York 10001 USA

Reprinted 2013

Produced by TAJ Books International LLC
219 Great Lake Drive
Cary, NC 27519, USA
www.tajbooks.com

Copyright ©2012 National Rifle Association of America

You can join the NRA by contacting them at
The National Rifle Association of America, 11250 Waples Mill Road, Fairfax, VA 22030
or by visiting their website, www.nra.org/museumoffer
And you can view the treasures of the NRA National Firearms Museum at www.nramuseum.com.
The museum is open every day of the week, except Christmas day, at NRA Headquarters in Fairfax, VA,
near Washington DC. There is no admission charge.

All notations of errors or omissions should be addressed to TAJ Books, 113E Melbourne Park Circle,
Charlottesville, VA 22901, USA, info@tajbooks.com.

ISBN-13: 978-0-7858-2990-4
ISBN-10: 0-7858-2990-3

Library of Congress Cataloging-in-Publication Data available on request.

Printed in China.

2 3 4 5 16 15 14 13

NRA National Firearms Museum Staff: Director Jim Supica. Senior Curators Philip Schreier & Doug Wicklund.
Store Manager Benjamin Van Scoyoc. Administrative Assistant Sylvia Schneider. Senior Special Projects Coordinator Caroline Simms.
Curator Programs Matt Sharpe. Curator Collections Amber Lammers.

CONTENTS

HOW TO USE THIS BOOK

This Gun Collector's Logbook is designed to provide a convenient source for firearms collectors and enthusiasts to keep an orderly and informative record of their collection. It is also designed so that it may fulfill the role of a "bound book" for collectors who choose to apply for and maintain a collector's Federal Firearms License (FFL).

Firearm Collector's Acquisition and Disposition Record – The boxes on each page that include "Description of Firearm," "Receipt," and "Disposition" use the specific language specified in Table 5 of Title 27 CRF Chapter II, Part 478, as of this writing. A collector's license is not required to collect firearms, but it does provide some advantages in methods of acquiring certain types of firearms known as "Curios & Relics" (C&R). More information on the Collector's FFL may be found on page 94.

Important Disclaimer – Nothing in this book should be considered legal advice. It is the responsibility of the individual collector to determine that his activities and recordkeeping are in compliance with all applicable laws and regulations. It is the responsibility of the individual FFL holder to read, understand, and follow all applicable laws and regulations and to determine that his method of recordkeeping meets all current requirements. This book is not guaranteed to meet any specific requirements. Also note that laws and regulations may have changed since the publication of this book and that there may be additional state or local laws that affect the individual firearms collector that are beyond the scope of these few pages. However, we hope that this book will be useful in providing preliminary guidance for the collector's personal research to conduct his hobby in an enjoyable, legal, and responsible manner.

Collection Notes – The bottom half of each record page is designed to help collectors keep personal notes that add to the understanding and enjoyment of the firearms in their collection. How this portion of the form is used is up to the individual collector's preferences. The various elements of the logbook include:

- Variation – Many guns have a variation that further distinguishes them, such as "1st type," "2nd Model," "Target Model," etc.
- Value estimates at acquisition & disposition – Amount paid for the gun and amount the gun was sold for
- Condition – Many collectors prefer to use the NRA Condition Terms: "Excellent," "Good," etc. See page 7 for definitions.
- Circa – Date the gun was manufactured (may be estimated or approximate).
- Attachments, related items – Scope, spare magazines, case, and accoutrements, etc.
- Finish type – Usually blue, nickel, or stainless. May wish to note refinish or restoration here.
- Percent coverage – An alternative method of rating a firearm's condition is to note the approximate percentage of original finish remaining.
- Grips or stock – May include substance (walnut, rubber, ivory, etc.) and description (Monte Carlo, full stock, target grips, etc.)
- Modifications – Refinish, customization, etc.
- Notes & Comments – Anything that is important to you about the firearm. Is there any history associated with this specific gun? Is there supporting documentation? Does it have a family history? Does this model have some historical significance or special usage? What makes this gun interesting or unique? Is there someone you want to have this gun at some time in the future or would you like it donated? (A helpful hint – the NRA and the National Firearms Museum always welcome donations of firearms!)
- Value estimates & dates – Many collectors like to track the value of their arms over time. This can be especially helpful to heirs who may be called upon to liquidate a collection after the collector's passing. Space is provided for estimated dollar value and year of estimate.

Example:
$ _ 1,000 2012 $ ___ 1,250 2014 $ ___ 1,400 2017 and so forth

FIREARMS SAFETY

The cornerstone of responsible firearms ownership is safety. The thoughtful collector will know the three basic NRA firearms safety rules by heart and will be sure that anyone who handles his collection knows them as well:

1. <u>ALWAYS</u> keep the gun pointed in a safe direction.

2. <u>ALWAYS</u> keep your finger off the trigger until ready to shoot.

3. <u>ALWAYS</u> keep the gun unloaded until ready to use.

Beyond the "Big Three" there are other vital safety procedures. When using or storing a gun, always follow these NRA rules:

• Know your target and what is beyond.

• Know how to use the gun safely.

• Be sure the gun is safe to operate.

• Use only the correct ammunition for your gun.

• Wear eye and ear protection as appropriate.

• Never use alcohol or drugs before or while shooting.

• Store guns so they are not accessible to unauthorized persons.

• Be aware that certain types of guns and many shooting activities require additional safety precautions.

Children seem to have a natural curiosity about guns, and it's never too early to begin teaching firearms safety to children. The NRA Eddie Eagle program has developed a set of safety rules that even the youngest child can learn. If a child encounters a gun, he or she is taught to

Stop! Don't touch! Leave the area! Tell an adult!

Special safety concerns for gun collectors. Regular cleaning is important in order for your gun to operate correctly and safely. Before cleaning your gun, make absolutely sure that it is unloaded and that no ammunition is present in the cleaning area.

In many gun collector situations, one must guard against mental laxness regarding firearms safety. On a shooting range or in the hunting field or when handling a personal defense firearm, most experienced gun owners know by heart to "treat every gun as if it is loaded," and the accepted practice is to personally load check a gun when it first comes into your hands. Even after confirming that a gun is unloaded, the experienced gun handler will scrupulously avoid allowing the muzzle of the gun to point at any individual or in a dangerous direction and will keep his finger off the trigger.

However, in gun-collecting situations, such as attending a gun show or auction, or examining a collection, an unfortunate tendency by poorly trained individuals may be to overlook the basics of firearms safety—to assume that guns are unloaded and to treat them casually. This oversight is an invitation to tragedy. In some rare circumstances it may not be acceptable to manipulate the action to load check a collectible firearm that is in as-new pristine condition, since this may result in tiny wear marks that could impact the gun's condition rating. This makes it even more important to keep the muzzle pointed in a safe direction, and finger off the trigger. The responsible gun collector must follow the basic safety rules at all times.

RESEARCHING VALUES

Although there are no set prices for collectable firearms, a reasonable estimate can be made of their probable value, which can help the collector in deciding about acquiring or disposing of a particular gun. In most cases, the following factors will help in making an estimate of the value of the gun:

1. **Identification** – This is primarily the make and model of the gun and often the specific variation. Most modern firearms will be prominently marked with the manufacturer (make) and the model name. However, some older and antique guns may have limited marking or be unmarked. In those situations, the collector will have to resort to personal knowledge, the help of a more advanced collector in that field, or reference books to identify the gun. In the case of many collector firearms, a sub-variation of a model may make a significant difference in value. This can include design or marking variations during production, unusual barrel lengths or finishes, special configurations, or other deviations from standard production guns. Note that in most cases these variations must be factory original and not later modifications to positively impact the value.

2. **Condition** – An accurate assessment of the condition of a gun is essential in determining its probable value. Variations in condition can easily halve or double the value of a collectable firearm. One common method of describing condition is to use the NRA Firearms Condition Standards, listed on the facing page. Note that there are different condition standard definitions for Antique and Modern firearms.

Another widely used method of describing firearms condition is the percentage-of-finish method. As popularized by the *Blue Book of Gun Values,* this method relies on estimating the percentage of original factory finish remaining on the gun. It's important to note that this standard cannot be used to evaluate a refinished gun or a gun whose original finish has been removed or turned to patina.

3. **Special considerations** – On some firearms, unusual considerations such as decorative engraving, customization, special historical markings, or historic attribution may result in a significant increase in the gun's value. Likewise, other factors such as refinishing, sporterizing, alteration, mismatched or replaced parts, or poor-quality engraving may reduce the value.

GUN VALUE REFERENCES. There are a number of books that estimate firearms values. The following are of special interest:

1. Blue Book of Gun Values by Steve Fjestad. This excellent work is probably the most widely used price guide. It uses the percentage method of condition evaluation and is extensive and comprehensive in its listings. It is updated annually so be sure you are using a current edition.

2. Flayderman's Guide to Antique American Firearms and Their Values by Norm Flayderman. This work is indispensable for the identification of American-made firearms through the early 20th Century. It is only updated periodically so the user must check when the most recent edition was published and be aware that if more than a couple years ago, values have likely changed—usually risen—sometimes considerably.

3. Standard Catalog of Firearms, currently by Jerry Lee. This useful guide features pictures of many of the guns it lists and can be especially helpful in identifying guns for which the model may be unknown. The user must be careful to note, however, that this guide uses condition descriptions that sound very similar to the traditional NRA Standards, but defines them differently, which regrettably can result in confusion in relying on the value estimates. This book is updated annually. Related useful books from the same publisher include Standard Catalog of Military Firearms by Peterson (updated annually), and Standard Catalog of Smith & Wesson by Supica & Nahas (updated every few years, so check publication date and adjust values accordingly).

NRA MODERN FIREARMS CONDITION STANDARDS:

NEW: Not previously sold at retail; in same condition as current factory production.

PERFECT: In new condition in every respect. (Note: many collectors & dealers use "As New" to describe this condition.)

EXCELLENT: New condition; used but little; no noticeable marring of wood or metal; bluing perfect (except at muzzle or sharp edges).

VERY GOOD: In perfect working condition; no appreciable wear on working surfaces; no corrosion or pitting, only minor surface dents or scratches.

GOOD: In safe working condition; minor wear on working surfaces; no broken parts; no corrosion or pitting that will interfere with proper functioning.

FAIR: In safe working condition, but well worn; perhaps requiring replacement of minor parts or adjustments which should be indicated in advertisement; no rust, but may have corrosion pits which do not render article unsafe or inoperable.

NRA ANTIQUE FIREARMS CONDITION STANDARDS:

FACTORY NEW: All original parts; 100% original finish; in perfect condition in every respect, inside and out.

EXCELLENT: All original parts; over 80% original finish; sharp lettering, numerals, and design on metal and wood; unmarred wood; fine bore.

FINE: All original parts; over 30% original finish; sharp lettering, numerals, and design on metal and wood; minor marks in wood; good bore.

VERY GOOD: All original parts; none to 30% original finish; original metal surfaces smooth with all edges sharp; clear lettering, numerals, and design on metal; wood slightly scratched or bruised; bore disregarded for collectors' firearms.

GOOD: Some minor replacement parts; metal smoothly rusted or lightly pitted in places, cleaned or re-blued; principal letters, numerals, and design on metal legible; wood refinished, scratched, bruised or minor cracks repaired; in good working order.

FAIR: Some major parts replaced; minor replacement parts may be required; metal rusted, may be lightly pitted all over, vigorously cleaned or re-blued; rounded edges of metal and wood; principal lettering, numerals, and design on metal partly obliterated; wood scratched, bruised, cracked or repaired where broken; in fair working order or can be easily repaired and placed in working order.

POOR: Major and minor parts replaced; major replacement parts required and extensive restoration needed; metal deeply pitted; principal lettering, numerals and design obliterated, wood badly scratched, bruised, cracked or broken; mechanically inoperative; generally undesirable as a collector's firearm.

The cutoff date for Modern vs. Antique is not defined for these standards. Among collectors, the most widely used definition of "antique" is borrowed from the GCA of 68 which sets the cutoff date as Jan. 1, 1899. However, as it applies to the condition standards, many collectors, dealers, and auction houses seem to use the "Antique" standards in describing guns made well into the 20th Century.

CARING FOR YOUR COLLECTION

Most shooters and firearms enthusiasts are familiar with proper care of their modern guns, including cleaning after shooting, a light coat of oil or synthetic protectant on exposed metal surfaces, secure storage, and avoiding high humidity. When considering valuable antique and other rare guns kept primarily as collectable or historic pieces rather than for shooting, there are additional considerations for conservation.

The typical firearm is composed of both an inorganic component (metal, usually steel) and an organic component (wood). Too dry of an environment can crack wood stocks, while too-moist conditions can result in metal corrosion. Even the very materials that make up an object can directly contribute to its own destruction as some organic materials interact badly with some inorganics. These conditions must be carefully monitored.

For best long-term storage or exhibition, consistent conditions approaching 70 degrees Fahrenheit and 50% relative humidity are best. Data loggers, which record environmental conditions, can be obtained for continual monitoring. Storing items in a location where they will not receive excessive direct sunlight or artificial illumination is advisable. With the change of seasons, checking pieces for signs of corrosion or other problems such as the developing of cracks in the wooden stock is also advisable. Many collectors utilize lemon oil on end grain sections to prevent cracking.

Long-term light levels should be kept under 200 lux for most firearms and under 100 lux for pieces with sensitive case-hardening colors. Ultraviolet radiation (UV) levels should be under 10 mW/lux. Curatorial supply firms (such as Gaylord 800-448-6160) offer these monitoring instruments.

Protection of firearms is done by careful application of an inert coating of microcrystalline wax after cleaning. This protective coating of microcrystalline wax serves as a transparent barrier, protecting surfaces from ultraviolet radiation, atmospheric pollutants, moisture, and corrosive oils found on human skin. Wax works better than an oil or liquid which evaporates, providing little in the way of long-term protection. Objects treated with wax are best handled in the future with white cotton gloves to minimize loss of the wax layer.

The National Firearms Museum store (703-267-1614) sells Renaissance brand microcrystalline wax in two container sizes. It is recommended that a supply of clean white cotton gloves be used to apply and handle the treated pieces. The wax can be applied to all surfaces, inside and out.

Any leather accoutrements such as slings require special attention and require stabilization with additives that help balance changes in the acidity or alkalinity of the leather, which can result from prolonged exposure to light. Checking with a leather conservator may be necessary to determine the exact treatment needed on certain pieces with unusual tanning methods.

Storing any firearm requires careful consideration for security as well as conservation. Separating firearms to minimize physical contact such as rubbing/scratching is important, and an inert material such as ethafoam (closed-cell polymer) can also avoid the buildup or retention of moisture that cloth and rug liners can create in a closed environment with little air circulation. Storing any firearm inside a zippered "gun rug" is not recommended because the trapped moisture will cause rusting. Dehumidifiers for safes and storage vaults need to allow the collected water to exit, otherwise it will continue to cause issues.

NRA National Firearms Museum

Conserving our firearms treasures – Telling the story of Americans and our guns – Information and services for collectors.

Located at NRA Headquarters, 11250 Waples Mill Rd., Fairfax, VA 22030

NRAmuseum.com

The Gatling Gun display case in the Petersen Gallery. Note antique cartridge board display on walls.

NRA NATIONAL FIREARMS MUSEUM

The heart of our operation is the Museum itself. Here we have on exhibit 3,000 guns spanning more than six centuries, presenting America's most significant firearms ranging from a wheellock that came over on the Mayflower to a NYPD Officer's revolver recovered from the ashes of the World Trade Center. Inside the fifteen galleries are guns owned by presidents and kings, lawmen and outlaws, gold medal Olympic shooters, and everyday plinking hobbyists. Military displays present the arms used to win and defend American freedom from Concord Bridge through Gettysburg, Guadalcanal, and Khe Sahn to Operation Desert Storm. The museum is more popular than ever, with attendance more than doubling over the past five years. This popularity can in part be attributed to new exhibits that have opened recently.

The Robert E. Petersen Gallery displays 400 of the finest firearms from the world famous Petersen collection, representing the largest donation in NRA history. It has been called "the most amazing room of firearms on display anywhere." While the collection is remarkable in its diversity, it is perhaps most noted for the spectacular examples of firearms engraving on display, especially on some of the world's finest double barrel shotguns and double rifles. Other strong themes include historic arms, oddities and curiosa, and the world's largest collection of Gatling guns on public display.

NRA National Firearms Museum, Petersen Gallery: Original Colt factory display board (left),
H&R display for the 1876 Philadelphia Centennial Exposition (right), display case of firearms curiosa (center).

Details of engraving masterpieces from the Petersen Gallery (clockwise from top left): Game scene engraving by Fracassi on a pair of Famars shotguns; Barre engraving ca. 1902 on a Purdey shotgun presented by King Edward VII to the Shah of Persia; bulino style elephant on Beretta double rifle; gargoyle by Fracassi on Rizzini shotgun; mythological scenes by the Brown brothers on Holland & Holland shotgun.

11

The National Firearms Museum Hollywood Guns Exhibit features 120 actual guns used in movies and television over the past 80 years, from the first revolver John Wayne used on camera through guns from recent Academy Award Winners such as the silenced shotgun from "No Country for Old Men," and the Barrett .50 cal. from "Hurt Locker." Other favorites in the exhibit include the Sharps used by Tom Selleck in "Quigley Down Under," blasters and light sabers from "Star Wars," the Beretta pistol used both by Mel Gibson in "Lethal Weapon" and by Bruce Willis in "Die Hard," and the .44 Magnum S&W carried by Clint Eastwood in "Dirty Harry."

From the Hollywood Guns display in the William B. Ruger Gallery (clockwise from top left): Beretta pistol used by both Bruce Willis in "Die Hard" and Mel Gibson in "Lethal Weapon"; Remington shotgun with suppressor used by Javier Bardem in "No Country for Old Men"; cut-down Remington 870 and H&K pistol used by Denzel Washington in "The Book of Eli"; S&W Model 29 used by Clint Eastwood in "Dirty Harry."

100 Years of the 1911 Pistol illustrates the adoption of the U.S. Service Pistol and its historic service. On display from the early pistol trials that resulted in the adoption of the 1911 are four Savage .45 acp pistols (Colt's closest competitor in the trials, including serial numbers 1, 2, and 4), one of the .30 cal. Lugers issued to U.S. Cavalry units for testing, Grant Hammond .45 ACP s/n 1, and one of the Model 1907 .45 ACP Colt pistols made for the trials. Pistols used by Congressional Medal of Honor recipient Joe Foss and Navy Cross recipient Adm. Willis Lee are also on exhibit along with Texas Ranger 1911s.

Pivotal pistols from the U.S. Military pistol trials (clockwise from top left): Grant Hammond .45 ACP, s/n 1; one of four .45 ACP Savage Model 1911s made for the final round of competition with the Colt; Colt Model 1907 .45 ACP made exclusively for military trials; and one of the Lugers issued to U.S. Cavalry for testing.

Above: Theodore Roosevelt exhibit, under construction. Artifacts visible here include TR's desk set from his "summer Oval Office" at Sagamore Hill; the chair he used as Governor of New York; his personal gun cabinet; a lion rug taken by TR on safari; a Gatling Gun used in support of the Rough Riders at San Juan Hill; and the regimental flag of the 1st U.S. Volunteer Cavalry.

At right: TR's Stetson hat, Brooks Brothers tunic, and inscribed sword from the Spanish American War. This new exhibit at the NRA National Firearms Museum features numerous items owned by Theodore Roosevelt, president and recipient of both the Congressional Medal of Honor and the Nobel Peace Prize. The vast majority of the artifacts are on loan from the Sagamore Hill National Historic Site through the National Park Service.

Theodore Roosevelt: Trappings of an Icon features items owned by TR on loan from the Sagamore Hill National Historic Site. Highlights include a dozen of his personal firearms, the furniture and contents of his "summer Oval Office" from his Sagamore Hill library, original illustrations from the books he wrote and original bronzes from his home, along with a fascinating array of personal effects. Items from his Rough Rider days in the Spanish American War include the Brooks Brothers uniform tunic and the Stetson hat he wore, his inscribed sword, and the regimental flag of the 1st U.S. Volunteer Cavalry, along with a Gatling gun used in support of the Rough Riders at San Juan and Kettle Hills.

ADDITIONAL MUSEUM LOCATIONS

NRA National Sporting Arms Museum at Bass Pro. Opening in 2013, at the Bass Pro flagship store in Springfield, MO, this entirely new museum presents an unprecedented showcase of the arms and rich heritage of hunting, conservation, and freedom in America. Featured exhibits include a timeline of three centuries of sporting arms, exceptional custom and engraved guns, historical firearms, guns used in movies, and the firearms of Theodore Roosevelt and other famous individuals.

NRA Old West Museum at SASS Founders Ranch. This new mini-museum at Single Action Shooting Society Founders Ranch in New Mexico will feature exhibits of guns of the Old West during special events such as End of the Trail.

National Scouting Museum Century of Marksmanship display at the Scouting Museum in Irving, TX, celebrates 100 years of cooperation between NRA and BSA training America's youth in shooting and firearms safety.

On the road. The Museum's staff travel to around 40 off-site locations each year to present firearms exhibits and lectures at gun shows, sporting shows, shooting competitions, and other events.

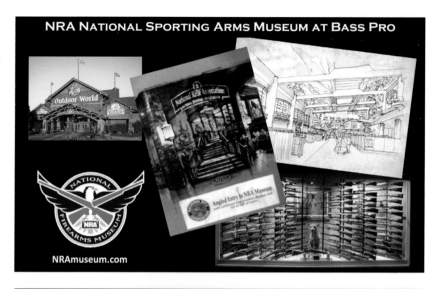

A MUSEUM WITHOUT WALLS

The Museum's educational program reaches millions via internet, television, and other media.

Television – The Museum is featured prominently on television, including on the most popular shows on specialty outdoorsman cable channels.

• **NRA's Guns & Gold** features Museum staff doing "Antique Road Show"-style evaluations of firearms on the Sportsman Channel.

• **Gun Stories with Joe Mantegna** on the Outdoors Channel tells the in-depth story of an iconic firearm model each week, with many of the interior shots filmed in the Museum with Museum staff featured as guest expert commentators.

• **American Rifleman Television** on the Outdoor Channel and **Cam & Co.** Curator's Corner on NRAtv.com and Sirius radio feature Museum guns and staff.

RESOURCES FOR COLLECTORS

• **NRAmuseum.com**, the National Firearms Museum website features 10,000 high-resolution zoomable photos of 3,000 guns and a special reference section for collectors and researchers with serial number tables and other essential references for gun collectors, along with articles on firearms and collecting.

• **YouTube** – The NFMcurator YouTube channel has over 300 videos on firearms history and gun collecting by the Museum. **youtube.com/NFMcurator**

• **Facebook** – Firearms enthusiasts can follow the Museum on their Facebook newsfeed by "liking" the NRA National Firearms Museum page. Fans of the NFM page enjoy spectacular, unusual, and historic firearms in the popular "Gun of the Day" post, along with the latest info from the Museum. **facebook.com/NRAmuseum**

• **Print** - *The Illustrated History of Firearms* (2011) features 1,500 guns from the Museum in full color. *Treasures of the NRA National Firearms Museum* (2013) presents full-page color photos of the finest guns in the Museum's collection, including masterpieces from the Petersen Gallery with engraving details. Both are available from the Museum Store at 703-267-1608.

• **Library** – Located in the Museum offices at NRA Headquarters, Fairfax, VA, the library is available to firearms researchers by appointment.

• **NRA National Gun Show** – Hosted by a different NRA Gun Collecting Affiliate in a new location around the country each year, the show offers cash awards for winning educational displays.

• **NRA Annual Meeting Display Competition** – Held at the NRA Annual Members Meeting, the competition presents outstanding educational displays by NRA-affiliated gun collecting clubs.

• **Night at the Museum** – Scout and other youth groups can request this special event that features an after-hours tour of the Museum, safety training, and hands-on examination of firearms.

• **The Museum Store** – Located next to the Museum, the Store features great NRA and Museum souvenirs, but better yet, has the best selection of firearms history and gun collector books to be found anywhere. See page 98.

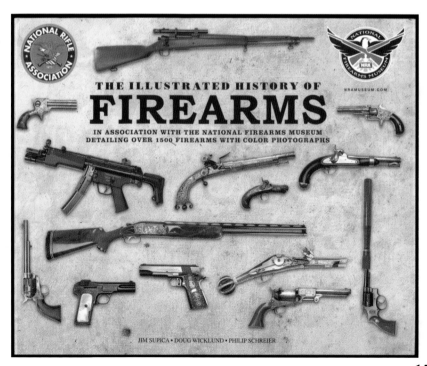

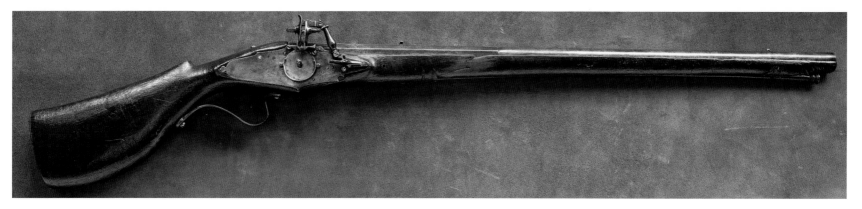

YOUR NRA NATIONAL FIREARMS MUSEUM

The Museum is supported by the members of the National Rifle Association and by donations to The NRA Foundation, a 501(c)(3) corporation. Of the thousands of guns in the museum, 99% have been donated over the past three quarters of a century by far-sighted individuals who understood the importance of telling the story of Americans and their firearms to this and future generations.

You can support the Museum by joining the NRA or by your donations. Firearms can be donated directly to the Museum or can be sold at auction to raise funds for the NRA program of your choice through the Firearms for Freedom program. Membership and donation information appears in the back pages of this book.

Above: Wheellock carbine brought over on the Mayflower by John Alden. Donated by the Alden family.

Left: Smith & Wesson revolver of Officer Walter Weaver who gave his life on Sept. 11, 2001, as recovered from the ashes of the World Trade Center. Donated by the Weaver family.

16

FIREARM COLLECTOR'S ACQUISITION AND DISPOSITION RECORD

Description of firearm				
Manufacturer and/or importer	Model	Serial No.	Type	Caliber or gauge

Receipt		Disposition				
Date	Name and address or name and license No.	Date	Name and address or name and license No.	Date of birth if nonlicensee	Driver's license No. or other identification if nonlicensee	For transfers to aliens, documentation used to establish residency

COLLECTION NOTES   Variation: _____ Value Estimate at Acquisition: $ _____ At Disposition: $ _____

Condition: _____ Circa: _____ Attachments, Related Items: _____

Finish Type: _____ Percent Coverage: _____ % Grips or Stock: _____ Modifications: _____

Notes & Comments:

Value Estimate & Date: $ _____ 20 ___ $ _____ 20 ___ $ _____ 20 ___ $ _____ 20 ___ $ _____ 20 ___

FIREARM COLLECTOR'S ACQUISITION AND DISPOSITION RECORD

Description of firearm				
Manufacturer and/or importer	Model	Serial No.	Type	Caliber or gauge

Receipt		Disposition				
Date	Name and address or name and license No.	*Date*	*Name and address or name and license No.*	*Date of birth if nonlicensee*	*Driver's license No. or other identification if nonlicensee*	*For transfers to aliens, documentation used to establish residency*

COLLECTION NOTES   Variation: _____ Value Estimate at Acquisition: $ _____ At Disposition: $ _____

Condition: _____ Circa: _____ Attachments, Related Items: _____

Finish Type: _____ Percent Coverage: _____ % Grips or Stock: _____ Modifications: _____

Notes & Comments:

Value Estimate & Date: $ _____ 20 ___ $ _____ 20 ___ $ _____ 20 ___ $ _____ 20 ___ $ _____ 20 ___

FIREARM COLLECTOR'S ACQUISITION AND DISPOSITION RECORD

Description of firearm				
Manufacturer and/or importer	Model	Serial No.	Type	Caliber or gauge

Receipt		Disposition				
Date	Name and address or name and license No.	*Date*	*Name and address or name and license No.*	*Date of birth if nonlicensee*	*Driver's license No. or other identification if nonlicensee*	*For transfers to aliens, documentation used to establish residency*

COLLECTION NOTES   Variation: _____ Value Estimate at Acquisition: $ _____ At Disposition: $ _____

Condition: _____ Circa: _____ Attachments, Related Items: _____

Finish Type: _____ Percent Coverage: _____ % Grips or Stock: _____ Modifications: _____

Notes & Comments:

Value Estimate & Date: $ _____ 20 ___ $ _____ 20 ___ $ _____ 20 ___ $ _____ 20 ___ $ _____ 20 ___

FIREARM COLLECTOR'S ACQUISITION AND DISPOSITION RECORD

Description of firearm				
Manufacturer and/or importer	Model	Serial No.	Type	Caliber or gauge

Receipt		Disposition				
Date	Name and address or name and license No.	*Date*	*Name and address or name and license No.*	*Date of birth if nonlicensee*	*Driver's license No. or other identification if nonlicensee*	*For transfers to aliens, documentation used to establish residency*

COLLECTION NOTES   Variation: _____ Value Estimate at Acquisition: $ _____ At Disposition: $ _____

Condition: _____ Circa: _____ Attachments, Related Items: _____

Finish Type: _____ Percent Coverage: _____ % Grips or Stock: _____ Modifications: _____

Notes & Comments:

Value Estimate & Date: $ _____ 20 ___ $ _____ 20 ___ $ _____ 20 ___ $ _____ 20 ___ $ _____ 20 ___

FIREARM COLLECTOR'S ACQUISITION AND DISPOSITION RECORD

Description of firearm				
Manufacturer and/or importer	Model	Serial No.	Type	Caliber or gauge

Receipt		Disposition				
Date	Name and address or name and license No.	Date	Name and address or name and license No.	Date of birth if nonlicensee	Driver's license No. or other identification if nonlicensee	For transfers to aliens, documentation used to establish residency

COLLECTION NOTES   Variation: _____ Value Estimate at Acquisition: $ _____ At Disposition: $ _____

Condition: _____ Circa: _____ Attachments, Related Items: _____

Finish Type: _____ Percent Coverage: _____ % Grips or Stock: _____ Modifications: _____

Notes & Comments:

Value Estimate & Date: $ _____ 20 ___ $ _____ 20 ___ $ _____ 20 ___ $ _____ 20 ___ $ _____ 20 ___

FIREARM COLLECTOR'S ACQUISITION AND DISPOSITION RECORD

Description of firearm				
Manufacturer and/or importer	Model	Serial No.	Type	Caliber or gauge

Receipt		Disposition				
Date	Name and address or name and license No.	*Date*	*Name and address or name and license No.*	*Date of birth if nonlicensee*	*Driver's license No. or other identification if nonlicensee*	*For transfers to aliens, documentation used to establish residency*

COLLECTION NOTES   Variation: _____ Value Estimate at Acquisition: $ _____ At Disposition: $ _____

Condition: _____ Circa: _____ Attachments, Related Items: _____

Finish Type: _____ Percent Coverage: _____ % Grips or Stock: _____ Modifications: _____

Notes & Comments:

Value Estimate & Date: $ _____ 20 ___ $ _____ 20 ___ $ _____ 20 ___ $ _____ 20 ___ $ _____ 20 ___

FIREARM COLLECTOR'S ACQUISITION AND DISPOSITION RECORD

Description of firearm				
Manufacturer and/or importer	Model	Serial No.	Type	Caliber or gauge

Receipt		Disposition				
Date	Name and address or name and license No.	Date	Name and address or name and license No.	Date of birth if nonlicensee	Driver's license No. or other identification if nonlicensee	For transfers to aliens, documentation used to establish residency

COLLECTION NOTES   Variation: _____ Value Estimate at Acquisition: $ _____ At Disposition: $ _____

Condition: _____ Circa: _____ Attachments, Related Items: _____

Finish Type: _____ Percent Coverage: _____ % Grips or Stock: _____ Modifications: _____

Notes & Comments:

Value Estimate & Date: $ _____ 20 ___ $ _____ 20 ___ $ _____ 20 ___ $ _____ 20 ___ $ _____ 20 ___

FIREARM COLLECTOR'S ACQUISITION AND DISPOSITION RECORD

Description of firearm				
Manufacturer and/or importer	Model	Serial No.	Type	Caliber or gauge

Receipt		Disposition				
Date	Name and address or name and license No.	Date	Name and address or name and license No.	Date of birth if nonlicensee	Driver's license No. or other identification if nonlicensee	For transfers to aliens, documentation used to establish residency

COLLECTION NOTES   Variation: _____ Value Estimate at Acquisition: $ _____ At Disposition: $ _____

Condition: _____ Circa: _____ Attachments, Related Items: _____

Finish Type: _____ Percent Coverage: _____ % Grips or Stock: _____ Modifications: _____

Notes & Comments:

Value Estimate & Date: $ _____ 20 ___ $ _____ 20 ___ $ _____ 20 ___ $ _____ 20 ___ $ _____ 20 ___

FIREARM COLLECTOR'S ACQUISITION AND DISPOSITION RECORD

Description of firearm				
Manufacturer and/or importer	Model	Serial No.	Type	Caliber or gauge

Receipt		Disposition				
Date	Name and address or name and license No.	*Date*	*Name and address or name and license No.*	*Date of birth if nonlicensee*	*Driver's license No. or other identification if nonlicensee*	*For transfers to aliens, documentation used to establish residency*

COLLECTION NOTES   Variation: _____ Value Estimate at Acquisition: $ _____ At Disposition: $ _____

Condition: _____ Circa: _____ Attachments, Related Items: _____

Finish Type: _____ Percent Coverage: _____ % Grips or Stock: _____ Modifications: _____

Notes & Comments:

Value Estimate & Date: $ _____ 20 ___ $ _____ 20 ___ $ _____ 20 ___ $ _____ 20 ___ $ _____ 20 ___

FIREARM COLLECTOR'S ACQUISITION AND DISPOSITION RECORD

Description of firearm				
Manufacturer and/or importer	Model	Serial No.	Type	Caliber or gauge

Receipt		Disposition				
Date	Name and address or name and license No.	*Date*	*Name and address or name and license No.*	*Date of birth if nonlicensee*	*Driver's license No. or other identification if nonlicensee*	*For transfers to aliens, documentation used to establish residency*

COLLECTION NOTES   Variation: _____   Value Estimate at Acquisition: $ _____   At Disposition: $ _____

Condition: _____   Circa: _____   Attachments, Related Items: _____

Finish Type: _____   Percent Coverage: _____ %   Grips or Stock: _____ Modifications: _____

Notes & Comments:

Value Estimate & Date: $ _____ 20 ___ $ _____ 20 ___ $ _____ 20 ___ $ _____ 20 ___ $ _____ 20 ___

FIREARM COLLECTOR'S ACQUISITION AND DISPOSITION RECORD

Description of firearm				
Manufacturer and/or importer	Model	Serial No.	Type	Caliber or gauge

Receipt		Disposition				
Date	Name and address or name and license No.	Date	Name and address or name and license No.	Date of birth if nonlicensee	Driver's license No. or other identification if nonlicensee	For transfers to aliens, documentation used to establish residency

COLLECTION NOTES   Variation: _____ Value Estimate at Acquisition: $ _____ At Disposition: $ _____

Condition: _____ Circa: _____ Attachments, Related Items: _____

Finish Type: _____ Percent Coverage: _____ % Grips or Stock: _____ Modifications: _____

Notes & Comments:

Value Estimate & Date: $ _____ 20 ___ $ _____ 20 ___ $ _____ 20 ___ $ _____ 20 ___ $ _____ 20 ___

FIREARM COLLECTOR'S ACQUISITION AND DISPOSITION RECORD

Description of firearm				
Manufacturer and/or importer	Model	Serial No.	Type	Caliber or gauge

Receipt		Disposition				
Date	Name and address or name and license No.	*Date*	*Name and address or name and license No.*	*Date of birth if nonlicensee*	*Driver's license No. or other identification if nonlicensee*	*For transfers to aliens, documentation used to establish residency*

COLLECTION NOTES   Variation: _____   Value Estimate at Acquisition: $ _____   At Disposition: $ _____

Condition: _____   Circa: _____   Attachments, Related Items: _____

Finish Type: _____   Percent Coverage: _____ %   Grips or Stock: _____ Modifications: _____

Notes & Comments:

Value Estimate & Date: $ _____ 20 ___ $ _____ 20 ___ $ _____ 20 ___ $ _____ 20 ___ $ _____ 20 ___

FIREARM COLLECTOR'S ACQUISITION AND DISPOSITION RECORD

Description of firearm				
Manufacturer and/or importer	Model	Serial No.	Type	Caliber or gauge

Receipt		Disposition				
Date	Name and address or name and license No.	Date	Name and address or name and license No.	Date of birth if nonlicensee	Driver's license No. or other identification if nonlicensee	For transfers to aliens, documentation used to establish residency

COLLECTION NOTES   Variation: _____ Value Estimate at Acquisition: $ _____ At Disposition: $ _____

Condition: _____ Circa: _____ Attachments, Related Items: _____

Finish Type: _____ Percent Coverage: _____ % Grips or Stock: _____ Modifications: _____

Notes & Comments:

Value Estimate & Date: $ _____ 20 ___ $ _____ 20 ___ $ _____ 20 ___ $ _____ 20 ___ $ _____ 20 ___

FIREARM COLLECTOR'S ACQUISITION AND DISPOSITION RECORD

Description of firearm				
Manufacturer and/or importer	Model	Serial No.	Type	Caliber or gauge

Receipt		Disposition				
Date	Name and address or name and license No.	Date	Name and address or name and license No.	Date of birth if nonlicensee	Driver's license No. or other identification if nonlicensee	For transfers to aliens, documentation used to establish residency

COLLECTION NOTES   Variation: _____ Value Estimate at Acquisition: $ _____ At Disposition: $ _____

Condition: _____ Circa: _____ Attachments, Related Items: _____

Finish Type: _____ Percent Coverage: _____ % Grips or Stock: _____ Modifications: _____

Notes & Comments:

Value Estimate & Date: $ _____ 20 ___ $ _____ 20 ___ $ _____ 20 ___ $ _____ 20 ___ $ _____ 20 ___

FIREARM COLLECTOR'S ACQUISITION AND DISPOSITION RECORD

Description of firearm				
Manufacturer and/or importer	Model	Serial No.	Type	Caliber or gauge

Receipt		Disposition				
Date	Name and address or name and license No.	Date	Name and address or name and license No.	Date of birth if nonlicensee	Driver's license No. or other identification if nonlicensee	For transfers to aliens, documentation used to establish residency

COLLECTION NOTES   Variation: _____ Value Estimate at Acquisition: $ _____ At Disposition: $ _____

Condition: _____ Circa: _____ Attachments, Related Items: _____

Finish Type: _____ Percent Coverage: _____ % Grips or Stock: _____ Modifications: _____

Notes & Comments:

Value Estimate & Date: $ _____ 20 ___ $ _____ 20 ___ $ _____ 20 ___ $ _____ 20 ___ $ _____ 20 ___

FIREARM COLLECTOR'S ACQUISITION AND DISPOSITION RECORD

Description of firearm				
Manufacturer and/or importer	Model	Serial No.	Type	Caliber or gauge

Receipt		Disposition				
Date	Name and address or name and license No.	*Date*	*Name and address or name and license No.*	*Date of birth if nonlicensee*	*Driver's license No. or other identification if nonlicensee*	*For transfers to aliens, documentation used to establish residency*

COLLECTION NOTES   Variation: _____ Value Estimate at Acquisition: $ _____ At Disposition: $ _____

Condition: _____ Circa: _____ Attachments, Related Items: _____

Finish Type: _____ Percent Coverage: _____ % Grips or Stock: _____ Modifications: _____

Notes & Comments:

Value Estimate & Date: $ _____ 20 ___ $ _____ 20 ___ $ _____ 20 ___ $ _____ 20 ___ $ _____ 20 ___

FIREARM COLLECTOR'S ACQUISITION AND DISPOSITION RECORD

Description of firearm				
Manufacturer and/or importer	Model	Serial No.	Type	Caliber or gauge

Receipt		Disposition				
Date	Name and address or name and license No.	*Date*	*Name and address or name and license No.*	*Date of birth if nonlicensee*	*Driver's license No. or other identification if nonlicensee*	*For transfers to aliens, documentation used to establish residency*

COLLECTION NOTES   Variation: _____ Value Estimate at Acquisition: $ _____ At Disposition: $ _____

Condition: _____ Circa: _____ Attachments, Related Items: _____

Finish Type: _____ Percent Coverage: _____ % Grips or Stock: _____ Modifications: _____

Notes & Comments:

Value Estimate & Date: $ _____ 20 ___ $ _____ 20 ___ $ _____ 20 ___ $ _____ 20 ___ $ _____ 20 ___

FIREARM COLLECTOR'S ACQUISITION AND DISPOSITION RECORD

Description of firearm				
Manufacturer and/or importer	Model	Serial No.	Type	Caliber or gauge

Receipt		Disposition				
Date	Name and address or name and license No.	*Date*	*Name and address or name and license No.*	*Date of birth if nonlicensee*	*Driver's license No. or other identification if nonlicensee*	*For transfers to aliens, documentation used to establish residency*

COLLECTION NOTES   Variation: _____ Value Estimate at Acquisition: $ _____ At Disposition: $ _____

Condition: _____ Circa: _____ Attachments, Related Items: _____

Finish Type: _____ Percent Coverage: _____ % Grips or Stock: _____ Modifications: _____

Notes & Comments:

Value Estimate & Date: $ _____ 20 ___ $ _____ 20 ___ $ _____ 20 ___ $ _____ 20 ___ $ _____ 20 ___

FIREARM COLLECTOR'S ACQUISITION AND DISPOSITION RECORD

Description of firearm				
Manufacturer and/or importer	Model	Serial No.	Type	Caliber or gauge

Receipt		Disposition				
Date	Name and address or name and license No.	Date	Name and address or name and license No.	Date of birth if nonlicensee	Driver's license No. or other identification if nonlicensee	For transfers to aliens, documentation used to establish residency

COLLECTION NOTES   Variation: _____ Value Estimate at Acquisition: $ _____ At Disposition: $ _____

Condition: _____ Circa: _____ Attachments, Related Items: _____

Finish Type: _____ Percent Coverage: _____ % Grips or Stock: _____ Modifications: _____

Notes & Comments:

Value Estimate & Date: $ _____ 20 __ $ _____ 20 __ $ _____ 20 __ $ _____ 20 __ $ _____ 20 __

FIREARM COLLECTOR'S ACQUISITION AND DISPOSITION RECORD

Description of firearm				
Manufacturer and/or importer	Model	Serial No.	Type	Caliber or gauge

Receipt		Disposition				
Date	Name and address or name and license No.	Date	Name and address or name and license No.	Date of birth if nonlicensee	Driver's license No. or other identification if nonlicensee	For transfers to aliens, documentation used to establish residency

COLLECTION NOTES   Variation: _____ Value Estimate at Acquisition: $ _____ At Disposition: $ _____

Condition: _____ Circa: _____ Attachments, Related Items: _____

Finish Type: _____ Percent Coverage: _____ % Grips or Stock: _____ Modifications: _____

Notes & Comments:

Value Estimate & Date: $ _____ 20 ___ $ _____ 20 ___ $ _____ 20 ___ $ _____ 20 ___ $ _____ 20 ___

FIREARM COLLECTOR'S ACQUISITION AND DISPOSITION RECORD

Description of firearm				
Manufacturer and/or importer	Model	Serial No.	Type	Caliber or gauge

Receipt		Disposition				
Date	Name and address or name and license No.	Date	Name and address or name and license No.	Date of birth if nonlicensee	Driver's license No. or other identification if nonlicensee	For transfers to aliens, documentation used to establish residency

COLLECTION NOTES   Variation: _____ Value Estimate at Acquisition: $ _____ At Disposition: $ _____

Condition: _____ Circa: _____ Attachments, Related Items: _____

Finish Type: _____ Percent Coverage: _____ % Grips or Stock: _____ Modifications: _____

Notes & Comments:

Value Estimate & Date: $ _____ 20 ___ $ _____ 20 ___ $ _____ 20 ___ $ _____ 20 ___ $ _____ 20 ___

FIREARM COLLECTOR'S ACQUISITION AND DISPOSITION RECORD

Description of firearm				
Manufacturer and/or importer	Model	Serial No.	Type	Caliber or gauge

Receipt		Disposition				
Date	Name and address or name and license No.	Date	Name and address or name and license No.	Date of birth if nonlicensee	Driver's license No. or other identification if nonlicensee	For transfers to aliens, documentation used to establish residency

COLLECTION NOTES   Variation: _____ Value Estimate at Acquisition: $ _____ At Disposition: $ _____

Condition: _____ Circa: _____ Attachments, Related Items: _____

Finish Type: _____ Percent Coverage: _____ % Grips or Stock: _____ Modifications: _____

Notes & Comments:

Value Estimate & Date: $ _____ 20 __ $ _____ 20 __ $ _____ 20 __ $ _____ 20 __ $ _____ 20 __

FIREARM COLLECTOR'S ACQUISITION AND DISPOSITION RECORD

Description of firearm				
Manufacturer and/or importer	Model	Serial No.	Type	Caliber or gauge

Receipt		Disposition				
Date	Name and address or name and license No.	Date	Name and address or name and license No.	Date of birth if nonlicensee	Driver's license No. or other identification if nonlicensee	For transfers to aliens, documentation used to establish residency

COLLECTION NOTES   Variation: _____ Value Estimate at Acquisition: $ _____ At Disposition: $ _____

Condition: _____ Circa: _____ Attachments, Related Items: _____

Finish Type: _____ Percent Coverage: _____ % Grips or Stock: _____ Modifications: _____

Notes & Comments:

Value Estimate & Date: $ _____ 20 ___ $ _____ 20 ___ $ _____ 20 ___ $ _____ 20 ___ $ _____ 20 ___

FIREARM COLLECTOR'S ACQUISITION AND DISPOSITION RECORD

Description of firearm				
Manufacturer and/or importer	Model	Serial No.	Type	Caliber or gauge

Receipt		Disposition				
Date	Name and address or name and license No.	*Date*	*Name and address or name and license No.*	*Date of birth if nonlicensee*	*Driver's license No. or other identification if nonlicensee*	*For transfers to aliens, documentation used to establish residency*

COLLECTION NOTES   Variation: _____ Value Estimate at Acquisition: $ _____ At Disposition: $ _____

Condition: _____ Circa: _____ Attachments, Related Items: _____

Finish Type: _____ Percent Coverage: _____ %   Grips or Stock: _____ Modifications: _____

Notes & Comments:

Value Estimate & Date: $ _____ 20 ___ $ _____ 20 ___ $ _____ 20 ___ $ _____ 20 ___ $ _____ 20 ___

FIREARM COLLECTOR'S ACQUISITION AND DISPOSITION RECORD

Description of firearm				
Manufacturer and/or importer	Model	Serial No.	Type	Caliber or gauge

Receipt		Disposition				
Date	Name and address or name and license No.	Date	Name and address or name and license No.	Date of birth if nonlicensee	Driver's license No. or other identification if nonlicensee	For transfers to aliens, documentation used to establish residency

COLLECTION NOTES   Variation: _____ Value Estimate at Acquisition: $ _____ At Disposition: $ _____

Condition: _____ Circa: _____ Attachments, Related Items: _____

Finish Type: _____ Percent Coverage: _____ %   Grips or Stock: _____ Modifications: _____

Notes & Comments:

Value Estimate & Date: $ _____ 20 ___ $ _____ 20 ___ $ _____ 20 ___ $ _____ 20 ___ $ _____ 20 ___

FIREARM COLLECTOR'S ACQUISITION AND DISPOSITION RECORD

Description of firearm				
Manufacturer and/or importer	Model	Serial No.	Type	Caliber or gauge

Receipt		Disposition				
Date	Name and address or name and license No.	*Date*	*Name and address or name and license No.*	*Date of birth if nonlicensee*	*Driver's license No. or other identification if nonlicensee*	*For transfers to aliens, documentation used to establish residency*

COLLECTION NOTES   Variation: _____ Value Estimate at Acquisition: $ _____ At Disposition: $ _____

Condition: _____ Circa: _____ Attachments, Related Items: _____

Finish Type: _____ Percent Coverage: _____ % Grips or Stock: _____ Modifications: _____

Notes & Comments:

Value Estimate & Date: $ _____ 20 ___ $ _____ 20 ___ $ _____ 20 ___ $ _____ 20 ___ $ _____ 20 ___

FIREARM COLLECTOR'S ACQUISITION AND DISPOSITION RECORD

Description of firearm				
Manufacturer and/or importer	Model	Serial No.	Type	Caliber or gauge

Receipt		Disposition				
Date	Name and address or name and license No.	Date	Name and address or name and license No.	Date of birth if nonlicensee	Driver's license No. or other identification if nonlicensee	For transfers to aliens, documentation used to establish residency

COLLECTION NOTES   Variation: _____ Value Estimate at Acquisition: $ _____ At Disposition: $ _____

Condition: _____ Circa: _____ Attachments, Related Items: _____

Finish Type: _____ Percent Coverage: _____ % Grips or Stock: _____ Modifications: _____

Notes & Comments:

Value Estimate & Date: $ _____ 20 ___ $ _____ 20 ___ $ _____ 20 ___ $ _____ 20 ___ $ _____ 20 ___

FIREARM COLLECTOR'S ACQUISITION AND DISPOSITION RECORD

Description of firearm				
Manufacturer and/or importer	Model	Serial No.	Type	Caliber or gauge

Receipt		Disposition				
Date	Name and address or name and license No.	*Date*	*Name and address or name and license No.*	*Date of birth if nonlicensee*	*Driver's license No. or other identification if nonlicensee*	*For transfers to aliens, documentation used to establish residency*

COLLECTION NOTES   Variation: _____   Value Estimate at Acquisition: $ _____   At Disposition: $ _____

Condition: _____   Circa: _____   Attachments, Related Items: _____

Finish Type: _____   Percent Coverage: _____ %   Grips or Stock: _____   Modifications: _____

Notes & Comments:

Value Estimate & Date: $ _____ 20 ____ $ _____ 20 ____ $ _____ 20 ____ $ _____ 20 ____ $ _____ 20 ____

FIREARM COLLECTOR'S ACQUISITION AND DISPOSITION RECORD

Description of firearm				
Manufacturer and/or importer	Model	Serial No.	Type	Caliber or gauge

Receipt		Disposition				
Date	Name and address or name and license No.	Date	Name and address or name and license No.	Date of birth if nonlicensee	Driver's license No. or other identification if nonlicensee	For transfers to aliens, documentation used to establish residency

COLLECTION NOTES   Variation: _____ Value Estimate at Acquisition: $ _____ At Disposition: $ _____

Condition: _____ Circa: _____ Attachments, Related Items: _____

Finish Type: _____ Percent Coverage: _____ % Grips or Stock: _____ Modifications: _____

Notes & Comments:

Value Estimate & Date: $ _____ 20 ___ $ _____ 20 ___ $ _____ 20 ___ $ _____ 20 ___ $ _____ 20 ___

FIREARM COLLECTOR'S ACQUISITION AND DISPOSITION RECORD

Description of firearm				
Manufacturer and/or importer	Model	Serial No.	Type	Caliber or gauge

Receipt		Disposition				
Date	Name and address or name and license No.	Date	Name and address or name and license No.	Date of birth if nonlicensee	Driver's license No. or other identification if nonlicensee	For transfers to aliens, documentation used to establish residency

COLLECTION NOTES   Variation: _____ Value Estimate at Acquisition: $ _____ At Disposition: $ _____

Condition: _____ Circa: _____ Attachments, Related Items: _____

Finish Type: _____ Percent Coverage: _____ % Grips or Stock: _____ Modifications: _____

Notes & Comments:

Value Estimate & Date: $ _____ 20 ___ $ _____ 20 ___ $ _____ 20 ___ $ _____ 20 ___ $ _____ 20 ___

FIREARM COLLECTOR'S ACQUISITION AND DISPOSITION RECORD

Description of firearm				
Manufacturer and/or importer	Model	Serial No.	Type	Caliber or gauge

Receipt		Disposition				
Date	Name and address or name and license No.	Date	Name and address or name and license No.	Date of birth if nonlicensee	Driver's license No. or other identification if nonlicensee	For transfers to aliens, documentation used to establish residency

COLLECTION NOTES   Variation: _____   Value Estimate at Acquisition: $ _____   At Disposition: $ _____

Condition: _____   Circa: _____   Attachments, Related Items: _____

Finish Type: _____   Percent Coverage: _____ %   Grips or Stock: _____   Modifications: _____

Notes & Comments:

Value Estimate & Date: $ _____ 20 __ $ _____ 20 __ $ _____ 20 __ $ _____ 20 __ $ _____ 20 __

FIREARM COLLECTOR'S ACQUISITION AND DISPOSITION RECORD

Description of firearm				
Manufacturer and/or importer	Model	Serial No.	Type	Caliber or gauge

Receipt		Disposition				
Date	Name and address or name and license No.	Date	Name and address or name and license No.	Date of birth if nonlicensee	Driver's license No. or other identification if nonlicensee	For transfers to aliens, documentation used to establish residency

COLLECTION NOTES   Variation: _____ Value Estimate at Acquisition: $ _____ At Disposition: $ _____

Condition: _____ Circa: _____ Attachments, Related Items: _____

Finish Type: _____ Percent Coverage: _____ % Grips or Stock: _____ Modifications: _____

Notes & Comments:

Value Estimate & Date: $ _____ 20 ___ $ _____ 20 ___ $ _____ 20 ___ $ _____ 20 ___ $ _____ 20 ___

FIREARM COLLECTOR'S ACQUISITION AND DISPOSITION RECORD

Description of firearm				
Manufacturer and/or importer	Model	Serial No.	Type	Caliber or gauge

Receipt		Disposition				
Date	Name and address or name and license No.	*Date*	*Name and address or name and license No.*	*Date of birth if nonlicensee*	*Driver's license No. or other identification if nonlicensee*	*For transfers to aliens, documentation used to establish residency*

COLLECTION NOTES   Variation: _____ Value Estimate at Acquisition: $ _____ At Disposition: $ _____

Condition: _____ Circa: _____ Attach_____ated Items: _____

Finish Type: _____ Percent Cove_____ ____ % Grips or Stock: _____ Modifications: _____

Notes & Comments:

Value Estimate & Date: $ _____ 20 ___ $ _____ 20 ___ $ _____ 20 ___ $ _____ 20 ___ $ _____ 20 ___

49

FIREARM COLLECTOR'S ACQUISITION AND DISPOSITION RECORD

Description of firearm				
Manufacturer and/or importer	Model	Serial No.	Type	Caliber or gauge

Receipt		Disposition				
Date	Name and address or name and license No.	Date	Name and address or name and license No.	Date of birth if nonlicensee	Driver's license No. or other identification if nonlicensee	For transfers to aliens, documentation used to establish residency

COLLECTION NOTES   Variation: _____ Value Estimate at Acquisition: $ _____ At Disposition: $ _____

Condition: _____ Circa: _____ Attachments, Related Items: _____

Finish Type: _____ Percent Coverage: _____ % Grips or Stock: _____ Modifications: _____

Notes & Comments:

Value Estimate & Date: $ _____ 20 ___ $ _____ 20 ___ $ _____ 20 ___ $ _____ 20 ___ $ _____ 20 ___

FIREARM COLLECTOR'S ACQUISITION AND DISPOSITION RECORD

Description of firearm				
Manufacturer and/or importer	Model	Serial No.	Type	Caliber or gauge

Receipt		Disposition				
Date	Name and address or name and license No.	*Date*	*Name and address or name and license No.*	*Date of birth if nonlicensee*	*Driver's license No. or other identification if nonlicensee*	*For transfers to aliens, documentation used to establish residency*

COLLECTION NOTES   Variation: _____ Value Estimate at Acquisition: $ _____ At Disposition: $ _____

Condition: _____ Circa: _____ Attachments, Related Items: _____

Finish Type: _____ Percent Coverage: _____ % Grips or Stock: _____ Modifications: _____

Notes & Comments:

Value Estimate & Date: $ _____ 20 ___ $ _____ 20 ___ $ _____ 20 ___ $ _____ 20 ___ $ _____ 20 ___

FIREARM COLLECTOR'S ACQUISITION AND DISPOSITION RECORD

Description of firearm				
Manufacturer and/or importer	Model	Serial No.	Type	Caliber or gauge

Receipt		Disposition				
Date	Name and address or name and license No.	Date	Name and address or name and license No.	Date of birth if nonlicensee	Driver's license No. or other identification if nonlicensee	For transfers to aliens, documentation used to establish residency

COLLECTION NOTES   Variation: _____ Value Estimate at Acquisition: $ _____ At Disposition: $ _____

Condition: _____ Circa: _____ Attachments, Related Items: _____

Finish Type: _____ Percent Coverage: _____ % Grips or Stock: _____ Modifications: _____

Notes & Comments:

Value Estimate & Date: $ _____ 20 ___ $ _____ 20 ___ $ _____ 20 ___ $ _____ 20 ___ $ _____ 20 ___

FIREARM COLLECTOR'S ACQUISITION AND DISPOSITION RECORD

Description of firearm				
Manufacturer and/or importer	Model	Serial No.	Type	Caliber or gauge

Receipt		Disposition				
Date	Name and address or name and license No.	Date	Name and address or name and license No.	Date of birth if nonlicensee	Driver's license No. or other identification if nonlicensee	For transfers to aliens, documentation used to establish residency

COLLECTION NOTES   Variation: _____ Value Estimate at Acquisition: $ _____ At Disposition: $ _____

Condition: _____ Circa: _____ Attachments, Related Items: _____

Finish Type: _____ Percent Coverage: _____ % Grips or Stock: _____ Modifications: _____

Notes & Comments:

Value Estimate & Date: $ _____ 20 ___ $ _____ 20 ___ $ _____ 20 ___ $ _____ 20 ___ $ _____ 20 ___

FIREARM COLLECTOR'S ACQUISITION AND DISPOSITION RECORD

Description of firearm				
Manufacturer and/or importer	Model	Serial No.	Type	Caliber or gauge

Receipt		Disposition				
Date	Name and address or name and license No.	Date	Name and address or name and license No.	Date of birth if nonlicensee	Driver's license No. or other identification if nonlicensee	For transfers to aliens, documentation used to establish residency

COLLECTION NOTES   Variation: _____ Value Estimate at Acquisition: $ _____ At Disposition: $ _____

Condition: _____ Circa: _____ Attachments, Related Items: _____

Finish Type: _____ Percent Coverage: _____ % Grips or Stock: _____ Modifications: _____

Notes & Comments:

Value Estimate & Date: $ _____ 20 ___ $ _____ 20 ___ $ _____ 20 ___ $ _____ 20 ___ $ _____ 20 ___

FIREARM COLLECTOR'S ACQUISITION AND DISPOSITION RECORD

Description of firearm				
Manufacturer and/or importer	Model	Serial No.	Type	Caliber or gauge

Receipt		Disposition				
Date	Name and address or name and license No.	Date	Name and address or name and license No.	Date of birth if nonlicensee	Driver's license No. or other identification if nonlicensee	For transfers to aliens, documentation used to establish residency

COLLECTION NOTES   Variation: _____   Value Estimate at Acquisition: $ _____   At Disposition: $ _____

Condition: _____   Circa: _____   Attachments, Related Items: _____

Finish Type: _____   Percent Coverage: _____ %   Grips or Stock: _____   Modifications: _____

Notes & Comments:

Value Estimate & Date: $ _____ 20 ___ $ _____ 20 ___ $ _____ 20 ___ $ _____ 20 ___ $ _____ 20 ___

FIREARM COLLECTOR'S ACQUISITION AND DISPOSITION RECORD

Description of firearm				
Manufacturer and/or importer	Model	Serial No.	Type	Caliber or gauge

Receipt		Disposition				
Date	Name and address or name and license No.	Date	Name and address or name and license No.	Date of birth if nonlicensee	Driver's license No. or other identification if nonlicensee	For transfers to aliens, documentation used to establish residency

COLLECTION NOTES   Variation: _____ Value Estimate at Acquisition: $ _____ At Disposition: $ _____

Condition: _____ Circa: _____ Attachments, Related Items: _____

Finish Type: _____ Percent Coverage: _____ % Grips or Stock: _____ Modifications: _____

Notes & Comments:

Value Estimate & Date: $ _____ 20 ___ $ _____ 20 ___ $ _____ 20 ___ $ _____ 20 ___ $ _____ 20 ___

FIREARM COLLECTOR'S ACQUISITION AND DISPOSITION RECORD

Description of firearm				
Manufacturer and/or importer	Model	Serial No.	Type	Caliber or gauge

Receipt		Disposition				
Date	Name and address or name and license No.	Date	Name and address or name and license No.	Date of birth if nonlicensee	Driver's license No. or other identification if nonlicensee	For transfers to aliens, documentation used to establish residency

COLLECTION NOTES   Variation: _____ Value Estimate at Acquisition: $ _____ At Disposition: $ _____

Condition: _____ Circa: _____ Attachments, Related Items: _____

Finish Type: _____ Percent Coverage: _____ % Grips or Stock: _____ Modifications: _____

Notes & Comments:

Value Estimate & Date: $ _____ 20 ___ $ _____ 20 ___ $ _____ 20 ___ $ _____ 20 ___ $ _____ 20 ___

FIREARM COLLECTOR'S ACQUISITION AND DISPOSITION RECORD

Description of firearm				
Manufacturer and/or importer	Model	Serial No.	Type	Caliber or gauge

Receipt		Disposition				
Date	Name and address or name and license No.	Date	Name and address or name and license No.	Date of birth if nonlicensee	Driver's license No. or other identification if nonlicensee	For transfers to aliens, documentation used to establish residency

COLLECTION NOTES   Variation: _____ Value Estimate at Acquisition: $ _____ At Disposition: $ _____

Condition: _____ Circa: _____ Attachments, Related Items: _____

Finish Type: _____ Percent Coverage: _____ % Grips or Stock: _____ Modifications: _____

Notes & Comments:

Value Estimate & Date: $ _____ 20 ___ $ _____ 20 ___ $ _____ 20 ___ $ _____ 20 ___ $ _____ 20 ___

FIREARM COLLECTOR'S ACQUISITION AND DISPOSITION RECORD

Description of firearm				
Manufacturer and/or importer	Model	Serial No.	Type	Caliber or gauge

Receipt		Disposition				
Date	Name and address or name and license No.	*Date*	*Name and address or name and license No.*	*Date of birth if nonlicensee*	*Driver's license No. or other identification if nonlicensee*	*For transfers to aliens, documentation used to establish residency*

COLLECTION NOTES   Variation: _____ Value Estimate at Acquisition: $ _____ At Disposition: $ _____

Condition: _____ Circa: _____ Attachments, Related Items: _____

Finish Type: _____ Percent Coverage: _____ % Grips or Stock: _____ Modifications: _____

Notes & Comments:

Value Estimate & Date: $ _____ 20 ___ $ _____ 20 ___ $ _____ 20 ___ $ _____ 20 ___ $ _____ 20 ___

FIREARM COLLECTOR'S ACQUISITION AND DISPOSITION RECORD

Description of firearm				
Manufacturer and/or importer	Model	Serial No.	Type	Caliber or gauge

Receipt		Disposition					
Date	Name and address or name and license No.	Date	Name and address or name and license No.	Date of birth if nonlicensee	Driver's license No. or other identification if nonlicensee	For transfers to aliens, documentation used to establish residency

COLLECTION NOTES   Variation: _____ Value Estimate at Acquisition: $ _____ At Disposition: $ _____

Condition: _____ Circa: _____ Attachments, Related Items: _____

Finish Type: _____ Percent Coverage: _____ % Grips or Stock: _____ Modifications: _____

Notes & Comments:

Value Estimate & Date: $ _____ 20 ___ $ _____ 20 ___ $ _____ 20 ___ $ _____ 20 ___ $ _____ 20 ___

FIREARM COLLECTOR'S ACQUISITION AND DISPOSITION RECORD

Description of firearm				
Manufacturer and/or importer	Model	Serial No.	Type	Caliber or gauge

Receipt		Disposition				
Date	Name and address or name and license No.	*Date*	*Name and address or name and license No.*	*Date of birth if nonlicensee*	*Driver's license No. or other identification if nonlicensee*	*For transfers to aliens, documentation used to establish residency*

COLLECTION NOTES   Variation: _____   Value Estimate at Acquisition: $ _____   At Disposition: $ _____

Condition: _____   Circa: _____   Attachments, Related Items: _____

Finish Type: _____   Percent Coverage: _____ %   Grips or Stock: _____   Modifications: _____

Notes & Comments:

Value Estimate & Date: $ _____ 20 __ $ _____ 20 __ $ _____ 20 __ $ _____ 20 __ $ _____ 20 __

FIREARM COLLECTOR'S ACQUISITION AND DISPOSITION RECORD

Description of firearm				
Manufacturer and/or importer	Model	Serial No.	Type	Caliber or gauge

Receipt		Disposition				
Date	Name and address or name and license No.	*Date*	*Name and address or name and license No.*	*Date of birth if nonlicensee*	*Driver's license No. or other identification if nonlicensee*	*For transfers to aliens, documentation used to establish residency*

COLLECTION NOTES   Variation: _____ Value Estimate at Acquisition: $ _____ At Disposition: $ _____

Condition: _____ Circa: _____ Attachments, Related Items: _____

Finish Type: _____ Percent Coverage: _____ % Grips or Stock: _____ Modifications: _____

Notes & Comments:

Value Estimate & Date: $ _____ 20 ___ $ _____ 20 ___ $ _____ 20 ___ $ _____ 20 ___ $ _____ 20 ___

FIREARM COLLECTOR'S ACQUISITION AND DISPOSITION RECORD

Description of firearm				
Manufacturer and/or importer	Model	Serial No.	Type	Caliber or gauge

Receipt		Disposition				
Date	Name and address or name and license No.	Date	Name and address or name and license No.	Date of birth if nonlicensee	Driver's license No. or other identification if nonlicensee	For transfers to aliens, documentation used to establish residency

COLLECTION NOTES   Variation: _____ Value Estimate at Acquisition: $ _____ At Disposition: $ _____

Condition: _____ Circa: _____ Attachments, Related Items: _____

Finish Type: _____ Percent Coverage: _____ % Grips or Stock: _____ Modifications: _____

Notes & Comments:

Value Estimate & Date: $ _____ 20 ___ $ _____ 20 ___ $ _____ 20 ___ $ _____ 20 ___ $ _____ 20 ___

63

FIREARM COLLECTOR'S ACQUISITION AND DISPOSITION RECORD

Description of firearm				
Manufacturer and/or importer	Model	Serial No.	Type	Caliber or gauge

Receipt		Disposition				
Date	Name and address or name and license No.	Date	Name and address or name and license No.	Date of birth if nonlicensee	Driver's license No. or other identification if nonlicensee	For transfers to aliens, documentation used to establish residency

COLLECTION NOTES   Variation: _____ Value Estimate at Acquisition: $ _____ At Disposition: $ _____

Condition: _____ Circa: _____ Attachments, Related Items: _____

Finish Type: _____ Percent Coverage: _____ % Grips or Stock: _____ Modifications: _____

Notes & Comments:

Value Estimate & Date: $ _____ 20 __ $ _____ 20 __ $ _____ 20 __ $ _____ 20 __ $ _____ 20 __

FIREARM COLLECTOR'S ACQUISITION AND DISPOSITION RECORD

Description of firearm				
Manufacturer and/or importer	Model	Serial No.	Type	Caliber or gauge

Receipt		Disposition				
Date	Name and address or name and license No.	Date	Name and address or name and license No.	Date of birth if nonlicensee	Driver's license No. or other identification if nonlicensee	For transfers to aliens, documentation used to establish residency

COLLECTION NOTES   Variation: _____ Value Estimate at Acquisition: $ _____ At Disposition: $ _____

Condition: _____ Circa: _____ Attachments, Related Items: _____

Finish Type: _____ Percent Coverage: _____ % Grips or Stock: _____ Modifications: _____

Notes & Comments:

Value Estimate & Date: $ _____ 20 ___ $ _____ 20 ___ $ _____ 20 ___ $ _____ 20 ___ $ _____ 20 ___

FIREARM COLLECTOR'S ACQUISITION AND DISPOSITION RECORD

Description of firearm				
Manufacturer and/or importer	Model	Serial No.	Type	Caliber or gauge

Receipt		Disposition				
Date	Name and address or name and license No.	*Date*	*Name and address or name and license No.*	*Date of birth if nonlicensee*	*Driver's license No. or other identification if nonlicensee*	*For transfers to aliens, documentation used to establish residency*

COLLECTION NOTES   Variation: _____ Value Estimate at Acquisition: $ _____ At Disposition: $ _____

Condition: _____ Circa: _____ Attachments, Related Items: _____

Finish Type: _____ Percent Coverage: _____ % Grips or Stock: _____ Modifications: _____

Notes & Comments:

Value Estimate & Date: $ _____ 20 ___ $ _____ 20 ___ $ _____ 20 ___ $ _____ 20 ___ $ _____ 20 ___

FIREARM COLLECTOR'S ACQUISITION AND DISPOSITION RECORD

Description of firearm				
Manufacturer and/or importer	Model	Serial No.	Type	Caliber or gauge

Receipt		Disposition				
Date	Name and address or name and license No.	Date	Name and address or name and license No.	Date of birth if nonlicensee	Driver's license No. or other identification if nonlicensee	For transfers to aliens, documentation used to establish residency

COLLECTION NOTES   Variation: _____   Value Estimate at Acquisition: $ _____   At Disposition: $ _____

Condition: _____   Circa: _____   Attachments, Related Items: _____

Finish Type: _____   Percent Coverage: _____ %   Grips or Stock: _____   Modifications: _____

Notes & Comments:

Value Estimate & Date: $ _____ 20 ___ $ _____ 20 ___ $ _____ 20 ___ $ _____ 20 ___ $ _____ 20 ___

FIREARM COLLECTOR'S ACQUISITION AND DISPOSITION RECORD

Description of firearm				
Manufacturer and/or importer	Model	Serial No.	Type	Caliber or gauge

Receipt		Disposition				
Date	Name and address or name and license No.	*Date*	*Name and address or name and license No.*	*Date of birth if nonlicensee*	*Driver's license No. or other identification if nonlicensee*	*For transfers to aliens, documentation used to establish residency*

COLLECTION NOTES   Variation: _____   Value Estimate at Acquisition: $ _____   At Disposition: $ _____

Condition: _____   Circa: _____   Attachments, Related Items: _____

Finish Type: _____   Percent Coverage: _____ %   Grips or Stock: _____   Modifications: _____

Notes & Comments:

Value Estimate & Date: $ _____ 20 __ $ _____ 20 __ $ _____ 20 __ $ _____ 20 __ $ _____ 20 __

FIREARM COLLECTOR'S ACQUISITION AND DISPOSITION RECORD

Description of firearm				
Manufacturer and/or importer	Model	Serial No.	Type	Caliber or gauge

Receipt		Disposition				
Date	Name and address or name and license No.	*Date*	*Name and address or name and license No.*	*Date of birth if nonlicensee*	*Driver's license No. or other identification if nonlicensee*	*For transfers to aliens, documentation used to establish residency*

COLLECTION NOTES   Variation: _____ Value Estimate at Acquisition: $ _____ At Disposition: $ _____

Condition: _____ Circa: _____ Attachments, Related Items: _____

Finish Type: _____ Percent Coverage: _____ % Grips or Stock: _____ Modifications: _____

Notes & Comments:

Value Estimate & Date: $ _____ 20 ___ $ _____ 20 ___ $ _____ 20 ___ $ _____ 20 ___ $ _____ 20 ___

FIREARM COLLECTOR'S ACQUISITION AND DISPOSITION RECORD

Description of firearm				
Manufacturer and/or importer	Model	Serial No.	Type	Caliber or gauge

Receipt		Disposition				
Date	Name and address or name and license No.	Date	Name and address or name and license No.	Date of birth if nonlicensee	Driver's license No. or other identification if nonlicensee	For transfers to aliens, documentation used to establish residency

COLLECTION NOTES   Variation: _____ Value Estimate at Acquisition: $ _____ At Disposition: $ _____

Condition: _____ Circa: _____ Attachments, Related Items: _____

Finish Type: _____ Percent Coverage: _____ % Grips or Stock: _____ Modifications: _____

Notes & Comments:

Value Estimate & Date: $ _____ 20 ___ $ _____ 20 ___ $ _____ 20 ___ $ _____ 20 ___ $ _____ 20 ___

FIREARM COLLECTOR'S ACQUISITION AND DISPOSITION RECORD

Description of firearm				
Manufacturer and/or importer	Model	Serial No.	Type	Caliber or gauge

Receipt		Disposition				
Date	Name and address or name and license No.	Date	Name and address or name and license No.	Date of birth if nonlicensee	Driver's license No. or other identification if nonlicensee	For transfers to aliens, documentation used to establish residency

COLLECTION NOTES   Variation: _____ Value Estimate at Acquisition: $ _____ At Disposition: $ _____

Condition: _____ Circa: _____ Attachments, Related Items: _____

Finish Type: _____ Percent Coverage: _____ % Grips or Stock: _____ Modifications: _____

Notes & Comments:

Value Estimate & Date: $ _____ 20 ___ $ _____ 20 ___ $ _____ 20 ___ $ _____ 20 ___ $ _____ 20 ___

FIREARM COLLECTOR'S ACQUISITION AND DISPOSITION RECORD

Description of firearm				
Manufacturer and/or importer	Model	Serial No.	Type	Caliber or gauge

Receipt		Disposition				
Date	Name and address or name and license No.	*Date*	*Name and address or name and license No.*	*Date of birth if nonlicensee*	*Driver's license No. or other identification if nonlicensee*	*For transfers to aliens, documentation used to establish residency*

COLLECTION NOTES   Variation: _____ Value Estimate at Acquisition: $ _____ At Disposition: $ _____

Condition: _____ Circa: _____ Attachments, Related Items: _____

Finish Type: _____ Percent Coverage: _____ % Grips or Stock: _____ Modifications: _____

Notes & Comments:

Value Estimate & Date: $ _____ 20 ___ $ _____ 20 ___ $ _____ 20 ___ $ _____ 20 ___ $ _____ 20 ___

FIREARM COLLECTOR'S ACQUISITION AND DISPOSITION RECORD

Description of firearm				
Manufacturer and/or importer	Model	Serial No.	Type	Caliber or gauge

Receipt		Disposition				
Date	Name and address or name and license No.	Date	Name and address or name and license No.	Date of birth if nonlicensee	Driver's license No. or other identification if nonlicensee	For transfers to aliens, documentation used to establish residency

COLLECTION NOTES   Variation: _____ Value Estimate at Acquisition: $ _____ At Disposition: $ _____

Condition: _____ Circa: _____ Attachments, Related Items: _____

Finish Type: _____ Percent Coverage: _____ % Grips or Stock: _____ Modifications: _____

Notes & Comments:

Value Estimate & Date: $ _____ 20 ___ $ _____ 20 ___ $ _____ 20 ___ $ _____ 20 ___ $ _____ 20 ___

FIREARM COLLECTOR'S ACQUISITION AND DISPOSITION RECORD

Description of firearm				
Manufacturer and/or importer	Model	Serial No.	Type	Caliber or gauge

Receipt		Disposition				
Date	Name and address or name and license No.	*Date*	*Name and address or name and license No.*	*Date of birth if nonlicensee*	*Driver's license No. or other identification if nonlicensee*	*For transfers to aliens, documentation used to establish residency*

COLLECTION NOTES   Variation: _____ Value Estimate at Acquisition: $ _____ At Disposition: $ _____

Condition: _____ Circa: _____ Attachments, Related Items: _____

Finish Type: _____ Percent Coverage: _____ % Grips or Stock: _____ Modifications: _____

Notes & Comments:

Value Estimate & Date: $ _____ 20 ___ $ _____ 20 ___ $ _____ 20 ___ $ _____ 20 ___ $ _____ 20 ___

FIREARM COLLECTOR'S ACQUISITION AND DISPOSITION RECORD

Description of firearm				
Manufacturer and/or importer	Model	Serial No.	Type	Caliber or gauge

Receipt		Disposition				
Date	Name and address or name and license No.	Date	Name and address or name and license No.	Date of birth if nonlicensee	Driver's license No. or other identification if nonlicensee	For transfers to aliens, documentation used to establish residency

COLLECTION NOTES   Variation: _____ Value Estimate at Acquisition: $ _____ At Disposition: $ _____

Condition: _____ Circa: _____ Attachments, Related Items: _____

Finish Type: _____ Percent Coverage: _____ % Grips or Stock: _____ Modifications: _____

Notes & Comments:

Value Estimate & Date: $ _____ 20 ___ $ _____ 20 ___ $ _____ 20 ___ $ _____ 20 ___ $ _____ 20 ___

FIREARM COLLECTOR'S ACQUISITION AND DISPOSITION RECORD

Description of firearm				
Manufacturer and/or importer	Model	Serial No.	Type	Caliber or gauge

Receipt		Disposition				
Date	Name and address or name and license No.	*Date*	*Name and address or name and license No.*	*Date of birth if nonlicensee*	*Driver's license No. or other identification if nonlicensee*	*For transfers to aliens, documentation used to establish residency*

COLLECTION NOTES   Variation: _____ Value Estimate at Acquisition: $ _____ At Disposition: $ _____

Condition: _____ Circa: _____ Attachments, Related Items: _____

Finish Type: _____ Percent Coverage: _____ % Grips or Stock: _____ Modifications: _____

Notes & Comments:

Value Estimate & Date: $ _____ 20 ___ $ _____ 20 ___ $ _____ 20 ___ $ _____ 20 ___ $ _____ 20 ___

FIREARM COLLECTOR'S ACQUISITION AND DISPOSITION RECORD

Description of firearm				
Manufacturer and/or importer	Model	Serial No.	Type	Caliber or gauge

Receipt		Disposition				
Date	Name and address or name and license No.	Date	Name and address or name and license No.	Date of birth if nonlicensee	Driver's license No. or other identification if nonlicensee	For transfers to aliens, documentation used to establish residency

COLLECTION NOTES   Variation: _____ Value Estimate at Acquisition: $ _____ At Disposition: $ _____

Condition: _____ Circa: _____ Attachments, Related Items: _____

Finish Type: _____ Percent Coverage: _____ % Grips or Stock: _____ Modifications: _____

Notes & Comments:

Value Estimate & Date: $ _____ 20 ___ $ _____ 20 ___ $ _____ 20 ___ $ _____ 20 ___ $ _____ 20 ___

FIREARM COLLECTOR'S ACQUISITION AND DISPOSITION RECORD

Description of firearm				
Manufacturer and/or importer	Model	Serial No.	Type	Caliber or gauge

Receipt		Disposition				
Date	Name and address or name and license No.	Date	Name and address or name and license No.	Date of birth if nonlicensee	Driver's license No. or other identification if nonlicensee	For transfers to aliens, documentation used to establish residency

COLLECTION NOTES   Variation: _____   Value Estimate at Acquisition: $ _____   At Disposition: $ _____

Condition: _____   Circa: _____   Attachments, Related Items: _____

Finish Type: _____   Percent Coverage: _____ %   Grips or Stock: _____   Modifications: _____

Notes & Comments:

Value Estimate & Date: $ _____ 20 __ $ _____ 20 __ $ _____ 20 __ $ _____ 20 __ $ _____ 20 __

FIREARM COLLECTOR'S ACQUISITION AND DISPOSITION RECORD

Description of firearm				
Manufacturer and/or importer	Model	Serial No.	Type	Caliber or gauge

Receipt		Disposition				
Date	Name and address or name and license No.	*Date*	*Name and address or name and license No.*	*Date of birth if nonlicensee*	*Driver's license No. or other identification if nonlicensee*	*For transfers to aliens, documentation used to establish residency*

COLLECTION NOTES   Variation: _____ Value Estimate at Acquisition: $ _____ At Disposition: $ _____

Condition: _____ Circa: _____ Attachments, Related Items: _____

Finish Type: _____ Percent Coverage: _____ % Grips or Stock: _____ Modifications: _____

Notes & Comments:

Value Estimate & Date: $ _____ 20 ___ $ _____ 20 ___ $ _____ 20 ___ $ _____ 20 ___ $ _____ 20 ___

FIREARM COLLECTOR'S ACQUISITION AND DISPOSITION RECORD

Description of firearm				
Manufacturer and/or importer	Model	Serial No.	Type	Caliber or gauge

Receipt		Disposition				
Date	Name and address or name and license No.	Date	Name and address or name and license No.	Date of birth if nonlicensee	Driver's license No. or other identification if nonlicensee	For transfers to aliens, documentation used to establish residency

COLLECTION NOTES   Variation: _____ Value Estimate at Acquisition: $ _____ At Disposition: $ _____

Condition: _____ Circa: _____ Attachments, Related Items: _____

Finish Type: _____ Percent Coverage: _____ % Grips or Stock: _____ Modifications: _____

Notes & Comments:

Value Estimate & Date: $ _____ 20 ___ $ _____ 20 ___ $ _____ 20 ___ $ _____ 20 ___ $ _____ 20 ___

FIREARM COLLECTOR'S ACQUISITION AND DISPOSITION RECORD

Description of firearm				
Manufacturer and/or importer	Model	Serial No.	Type	Caliber or gauge

Receipt		Disposition				
Date	Name and address or name and license No.	*Date*	*Name and address or name and license No.*	*Date of birth if nonlicensee*	*Driver's license No. or other identification if nonlicensee*	*For transfers to aliens, documentation used to establish residency*

COLLECTION NOTES   Variation: _____   Value Estimate at Acquisition: $ _____   At Disposition: $ _____

Condition: _____   Circa: _____   Attachments, Related Items: _____

Finish Type: _____   Percent Coverage: _____ %   Grips or Stock: _____   Modifications: _____

Notes & Comments:

Value Estimate & Date: $ _____ 20 ___ $ _____ 20 ___ $ _____ 20 ___ $ _____ 20 ___ $ _____ 20 ___

FIREARM COLLECTOR'S ACQUISITION AND DISPOSITION RECORD

Description of firearm				
Manufacturer and/or importer	Model	Serial No.	Type	Caliber or gauge

Receipt		Disposition				
Date	Name and address or name and license No.	*Date*	*Name and address or name and license No.*	*Date of birth if nonlicensee*	*Driver's license No. or other identification if nonlicensee*	*For transfers to aliens, documentation used to establish residency*

COLLECTION NOTES   Variation: _____ Value Estimate at Acquisition: $ _____ At Disposition: $ _____

Condition: _____ Circa: _____ Attachments, Related Items: _____

Finish Type: _____ Percent Coverage: _____ % Grips or Stock: _____ Modifications: _____

Notes & Comments:

Value Estimate & Date: $ _____ 20 ___ $ _____ 20 ___ $ _____ 20 ___ $ _____ 20 ___ $ _____ 20 ___

FIREARM COLLECTOR'S ACQUISITION AND DISPOSITION RECORD

Description of firearm				
Manufacturer and/or importer	Model	Serial No.	Type	Caliber or gauge

Receipt		Disposition				
Date	Name and address or name and license No.	Date	Name and address or name and license No.	Date of birth if nonlicensee	Driver's license No. or other identification if nonlicensee	For transfers to aliens, documentation used to establish residency

COLLECTION NOTES   Variation: _____ Value Estimate at Acquisition: $ _____ At Disposition: $ _____

Condition: _____ Circa: _____ Attachments, Related Items: _____

Finish Type: _____ Percent Coverage: _____ % Grips or Stock: _____ Modifications: _____

Notes & Comments:

Value Estimate & Date: $ _____ 20 ___ $ _____ 20 ___ $ _____ 20 ___ $ _____ 20 ___ $ _____ 20 ___

FIREARM COLLECTOR'S ACQUISITION AND DISPOSITION RECORD

Description of firearm				
Manufacturer and/or importer	Model	Serial No.	Type	Caliber or gauge

Receipt		Disposition				
Date	Name and address or name and license No.	*Date*	*Name and address or name and license No.*	*Date of birth if nonlicensee*	*Driver's license No. or other identification if nonlicensee*	*For transfers to aliens, documentation used to establish residency*

COLLECTION NOTES   Variation: _____   Value Estimate at Acquisition: $ _____   At Disposition: $ _____

Condition: _____   Circa: _____   Attachments, Related Items: _____

Finish Type: _____   Percent Coverage: _____ %   Grips or Stock: _____   Modifications: _____

Notes & Comments:

Value Estimate & Date: $ _____ 20 ___ $ _____ 20 ___ $ _____ 20 ___ $ _____ 20 ___ $ _____ 20 ___

FIREARM COLLECTOR'S ACQUISITION AND DISPOSITION RECORD

Description of firearm				
Manufacturer and/or importer	Model	Serial No.	Type	Caliber or gauge

Receipt		Disposition				
Date	Name and address or name and license No.	*Date*	*Name and address or name and license No.*	*Date of birth if nonlicensee*	*Driver's license No. or other identification if nonlicensee*	*For transfers to aliens, documentation used to establish residency*

COLLECTION NOTES   Variation: _____   Value Estimate at Acquisition: $ _____ At Disposition: $ _____

Condition: _____ Circa: _____ Attachments, Related Items: _____

Finish Type: _____ Percent Coverage: _____ % Grips or Stock: _____ Modifications: _____

Notes & Comments:

Value Estimate & Date: $ _____ 20 ___ $ _____ 20 ___ $ _____ 20 ___ $ _____ 20 ___ $ _____ 20 ___

FIREARM COLLECTOR'S ACQUISITION AND DISPOSITION RECORD

Description of firearm				
Manufacturer and/or importer	Model	Serial No.	Type	Caliber or gauge

Receipt		Disposition				
Date	Name and address or name and license No.	Date	Name and address or name and license No.	Date of birth if nonlicensee	Driver's license No. or other identification if nonlicensee	For transfers to aliens, documentation used to establish residency

COLLECTION NOTES   Variation: _____ Value Estimate at Acquisition: $ _____ At Disposition: $ _____

Condition: _____ Circa: _____ Attachments, Related Items: _____

Finish Type: _____ Percent Coverage: _____ % Grips or Stock: _____ Modifications: _____

Notes & Comments:

Value Estimate & Date: $ _____ 20 ___ $ _____ 20 ___ $ _____ 20 ___ $ _____ 20 ___ $ _____ 20 ___

FIREARM COLLECTOR'S ACQUISITION AND DISPOSITION RECORD

Description of firearm				
Manufacturer and/or importer	Model	Serial No.	Type	Caliber or gauge

Receipt		Disposition				
Date	Name and address or name and license No.	*Date*	*Name and address or name and license No.*	*Date of birth if nonlicensee*	*Driver's license No. or other identification if nonlicensee*	*For transfers to aliens, documentation used to establish residency*

COLLECTION NOTES   Variation: _____ Value Estimate at Acquisition: $ _____ At Disposition: $ _____

Condition: _____ Circa: _____ Attachments, Related Items: _____

Finish Type: _____ Percent Coverage: _____ % Grips or Stock: _____ Modifications: _____

Notes & Comments:

Value Estimate & Date: $ _____ 20 ___ $ _____ 20 ___ $ _____ 20 ___ $ _____ 20 ___ $ _____ 20 ___

LIST OF NRA-AFFILIATED GUN COLLECTOR CLUBS

Alabama Gun Collectors Association
PO Box 242277
Montgomery, AL, 36124

Alabama Military Collectors Association, Inc.
PO Box 14001
Huntsville, AL, 35815

Alamo Antique Arms Association
19903 Encino Ridge
San Antonio, TX, 78259

Alaska Gun Collectors Association
P.O. Box 242233
Anchorage, AK, 99524

American Custom Gunmakers Guild
22 Vista View Lane
Cody, WY, 82414

American Single Shot Rifle Association
914 2nd Ave
Eau Claire, WI, 54703

American Society of Arms Collectors
P.O.Box 50400
Albuquerque, NM, 87181

Ark La Tex Gun Collectors Association, Inc.
180 Arthur Ave
Shreveport, LA, 71105

Arms Collectors of Georgia
4357 Highborne Drive
Marietta, GA, 30066

Arms Collectors of Southwest Washington
PO Box 2622
Vancouver, WA, 98668

Association of Ohio Longrifles Collectors
3321 West Point Rd, SE
Lancaster, OH, 43130

Bayou Gun Club of Louisiana, LA
4120 Ithica Street
Metairie, LA, 70002

Central Illinois Gun Collectors, Inc.
P. O. Box 462
Chatham, IL, 62629

Central PA Antique Arms Association
P.O.Box 914
Mechanicsburg, PA, 17055

Central Wisconsin Gun Collectors Association
W3085 Cicero Road
Seymour, WI, 54165

Collector Arms Dealers Association
P.O.Box 1074
Murrieta, CA, 92564

Colorado Gun Collectors Association
3490 E. Orchard Rd
Centennial, CO, 80121

Colt Collectors Association, Inc.
25000 Highland Way
Los Gatos, CA, 95033

Contemporary Longrifle Association
P.O. Box 2247
Staunton, VA, 24402

Continental Arms Collectors Association, Inc.
1126 County Route 20
Oswego, NY, 13126

Dakota Territory Gun Collectors Association, Inc.
P. O. Box 5053
West Fargo, ND, 58036

Dallas Arms Collectors Association, Inc.
9504 Winding Ridge Dr.
Dallas, TX 75238

Delaware Antique Arms Collectors Association, Inc.
PO Box 2966
Wilmington, DE, 19805

Eastern Shore Arms Collectors, Inc.
135 Chapel Road
Easton, MD, 21601

LIST OF NRA-AFFILIATED GUN COLLECTOR CLUBS

Egyptian Collectors Association, Inc.
PO Box 202
Hoffman, IL, 62250

Forks of Delaware Historical Arms Society, Inc.
2060 Northampton St. Unit 1
Easton, PA, 18042

German Gun Collectors Association
P.O. Box 429
Mayfield, UT, 84643

Glock Collectors Association
102 Playhouse Corner
Southbury, CT, 06488

Gulf Coast Gun Collectors Association
P.O. Box 2922
Daphne, AL, 36526

Hawaii Historic Arms Association
P.O. Box 1733
Honolulu, HI, 96806

Heritage Arms Society, Inc.
2412 E 114th St
Burnsville, MN, 55337

High Standard Collectors' Assn.
P. O. Box 1578
Decatur, IL, 62525

Houston Gun Collectors Association
P.O.Box 741429
Houston, TX, 77274

International Ammunition Association
996 Mason Woods Dr. NE
Atlanta, GA, 30329

Iroquois Arms & Collectors Association
1775 Swann Road
Randsomville, NY, 14131

Kentucky Rifle Association
8215 Overview Ct.
Roswell, GA, 30076

L C Smith Collectors Association
1322 Bay Ave
Mantoloking, NJ, 08738

L.I. Antique Historical Arms Society, Inc.
49 Avis Dr
East Meadow, NY, 11554

Lancaster Muzzleloading Club
37 Ridge Road
New Providence, PA, 17560

Mahoning Valley Gun Collectors Association
P. O. Box 86
Campbell, OH, 44405

Marlin Firearms Collectors Association
P.O. Box 491
Clay Center, KS, 67432

Maryland Arms Collectors Association
306 Amherst Ct.
Bel Air, MD, 21014

Massachusetts Arms Collectors, Inc.
P.O. Box 111
Hingman, MA 02043

Michigan Antique Arms Collectors
2454 Dorchester N.
Troy, MI, 48084

Miniature Arms Collectors and Makers Society, Ltd.
2109 Spring Street
Cross Plaines, WI, 53528

Missouri Arms Collectors Association
716 Lemay Ferry Road
St.Louis, MO, 63125

Missouri Valley Arms Collectors Associaton, Inc.
P. O. Box 13449
Edwardsville, KS, 66113

MN Weapons Collectors Association, Inc.
P.O.Box 605
Waseca, MN, 56093

LIST OF NRA-AFFILIATED GUN COLLECTOR CLUBS

National Auto Pistol Collection Association
P.O.Box 15738
St Louis, MO, 63163

National Mossberg Collectors Association
P.O.Box 487
Festus, MO, 63028

New England Antique Arms Society
PO Box 1030
Ashburnham, MA, 01430

New Mexico Gun Collectors Association
P.O.Box 66467
Albuquerque, NM, 87193

North Florida Arms Collectors Association, Inc.
614 Miramar Lane
Ponte Vedra, FL, 32082

Northeastern Arms Collectors Association, Inc.
P. O. BOX 185
AMITYVILLE, NY, 11701

Northern Indiana Gun Collectors Association
15237 W. 12th Road
Plymouth, IN, 46563

NW Montana Arms Collectors Association
P.O. Box 653
Kalispell, MT 59903

NY State Arms Collectors Association, Inc.
346 Paul Street
Endicott, NY, 13760

Ohio Gun Collectors Association, Inc.
PO Box 670406
Sagamore Hills, OH, 44067

Oregon Arms Collectors, Inc.
2221 NE Hoyt Street
Portland, OR, 97232

Orville Dunham Antique Gun Collectors
4040 E.Cerro Gordo Street
Decatur, IL, 62521

PA Gun Collectors Association
PO Box 246
Glenshaw, PA, 15116

Palm Beach Arms Collectors, Inc.
3611 Eastview Avenue
West Palm Beach, FL, 33407

Parker Gun Collectors Association
477 Ocean Ave
Wells, ME 04090

Penn Antique Gun Collectors Association
P.O. Box 97
Slatington, PA, 18080

Pioneer Gun Club of Michigan
10169 Gold Lake Rd
Belding, MI, 48809

Pioneer Gun Collectors Association
4500 South Georgia
Amarillo, TX, 79110

Potomac Arms Collector's Association
308 Colesville Manor Drive
Sliverspring, MD, 20904

Remington Society of America
71 Newton Ave
Glen Ellyn, IL, 60137

San Gabriel Valley Arms Collectors
1441 Deaubille Place
Costa Mesa, CA, 92626

San Luis Obispo Historical Arms Society
PO Box 81
Morro Bay, CA, 93443

Santa Barbara Historical Arms Association, Inc.
P.O.Box 6291
Santa Barbara, CA, 93160

Smith & Wesson Collectors Association
P. O. Box 378
Larned, KS, 67550

LIST OF NRA-AFFILIATED GUN COLLECTOR CLUBS

SC Arms Collectors Association, Inc.
P. O. Box 4308
Irmo, SC, 29063

South Jersey Arms Collectors
105 N Jefferson Ave
Wenonah, NJ, 08090

Southern California Arms Collectors Association
P.O.Box 7432
Thousand Oaks, CA, 91362

St. Louis Weapon Collectors
2854 Belle Terre Ct
St. Louis, MO, 63129

Stark Gun Collectors
1206 Orrville St, NW
Massillon, OH, 44647

Stratford Gun Collectors Association, Inc.
167 Dana Lane
Meriden, CT, 06451

Swiss Gun Collectors Association
18 Velie Ave
Barre, VT, 05641

Tenn. Military Association
P.O.Box 1006
Brentwood, TN, 37024

Texas Gun Collectors Association
131 Mittmann Circle
Canyon Lake, TX 78132

The American Thompson Association
P. O. Box 8710
Newark, OH, 43058

Thompson Collectors Association
P.O. Box 1675
Ellicott City, MD, 21041

Tri State Gun Collectors, Inc
P. O. Box 217, 912 Carnation
Wapakoneta, OH, 45895

Tulsa Arms Collectors Association
5110 S. Yale Ave #414
Tulsa, OK, 74153

Utah Gun Collectors Association
2247 N. Valley View Dr.
Layton, UT, 84040

VA Gun Collectors Association, Inc.
38802 Charles Town Pike
Waterford, VA, 20197

Washington Arms Collectors, Inc.
P.O. Box 389
Renton, WA, 98057

Weapons Collectors Society of Montana
7173 US Hwy 89 So.
Belt, MT, 59412

Weatherby Collectors Association, Inc.
P.O. Box 1217
Washington, MO, 63090

Westchester Collectors Club
43 Harbor Hills Dr
Port Washington, NY, 11050

Willamette Valley Arms Collectors Association
331 W. 13th Ave, Suite D
Eugene, OR, 97401

Winchester Arms Collectors Association
915 SW Rimrock Way, Ste 201-401
Redmond, OR, 97756

Wisconsin Gun Collectors Association, Inc.
P. O. Box 285
Menomonee Falls, WI, 53052

Wyoming Weapons Collectors
P. O. Box 1784
Laramie, WY, 82073

Ye Conn Gun Guild, Inc.
P.O. Box 373
Windsor, CT, 06095

Zumbro Valley Arms Collectors, Inc.
4138 32nd Street, SE
Rochester, MN, 55904

FEDERAL FIREARMS LAWS AND THE GUN COLLECTOR

Important disclaimer – The information below is intended to provide the collector with a very general introduction to a few of the legal requirements concerning his hobby. It is far from a complete discussion. Nothing in this book should be considered legal advice. It is the responsibility of the individual collector to determine that his activities are in compliance with all applicable laws and regulations. Consult an attorney for legal advice. This information is presented from a layman's perspective to introduce the firearms enthusiast to some basic concepts of the laws concerning firearms ownership and transfer and to provide some suggestions for further research. It is vitally important to remember that **laws and regulations change**, and what may have applied at the time of this writing may have changed by the time this is read. It is equally important to remember that there may be **state and local laws and regulations** that impact the firearms owner, and which vary from Federal law, which are beyond the scope of this discussion.

The Second Amendment: *"A well regulated militia being necessary to the security of a free state, the right of the people to keep and bear arms shall not be infringed."* The Second Amendment to the U.S. Constitution recognizes the individual right to keep and bear arms. Recent Supreme Court decisions have confirmed this right. District of Columbia v. Heller ruled that the Second Amendment protects the individual's right to possess a firearm, and McDonald v. Chicago ruled the Second Amendment applies to state and local governments as well as the Federal government.

Information on Federal laws and regulations. Current laws and regulations, along with answers to many questions, may be found at the website of the Bureau of Alcohol, Tobacco, Firearms and Explosives (ATF or BATFE) - **http://www.atf.gov/** . You can also order publications from the ATF, including Federal Firearms Regulations Reference Guide (the Questions & Answers section in the back of this book may be of special interest to gun collectors), State Laws and Published Ordinances – Firearms, and Firearms Curios or Relics List.

Buying Firearms from a dealer. Many collectors and shooters are familiar with the procedure for purchasing a modern firearm from a licensed firearms dealer. In most cases, the buyer fills out a form 4473 which contains identification information and states that the buyer does not fall in any of the classes of individuals who are prohibited from buying firearms. The buyer provides qualified identification documentation to the dealer (usually a state driver's license). The dealer then contacts the National Instant Criminal Background Check System (NICS) to confirm the eligibility of the buyer to purchase firearms. In most cases, the okay to purchase is provided immediately, but in some cases it may be delayed. In some areas, there are other state or local requirements for the purchase.

Federal Firearms License (FFL). The Federal government licenses certain activities with regards to firearms. A dealer's FFL is required to be in the business of dealing in firearms. Likewise, there are special FFL's for manufacturers and importers of firearms. Some collectors choose to keep a Collector's FFL, as discussed below.

Modern firearms and Antique firearms. The rules on the ownership and transfer of firearms contained in the Gun Control Act of 1968 do not apply to "Antique firearms." The definition of Antique firearm appears below. Note that guns made prior to Jan. 1, 1899, are considered to be "antiques" and are not covered by the GCA 68 regulations on ownership and transfer.

> **Antique firearm.**
> (a) Any firearm (including any firearm with a matchlock, flintlock, percussion cap, or similar type of ignition system) manufactured in or before 1898; and
> (b) any replica of any firearm described in paragraph (a) of this definition if such replica
>   (1) is not designed or redesigned for using rimfire or conventional centerfire fixed ammunition, or
>   (2) uses rimfire or conventional centerfire fixed ammunition which is no longer manufactured in the United States and which is not readily available in the ordinary channels of commercial trade.

(c) any muzzle loading rifle, muzzle loading shotgun, or muzzle loading pistol, which is designed to use black powder, or a black powder substitute, and which cannot use fixed ammunition. For purposes of this subparagraph, the term 'antique firearm' shall not include any weapon which incorporates a firearm frame or receiver, any firearm which is converted into a muzzle loading weapon, or any muzzle loading weapon, which can be readily converted to fire fixed ammunition by replacing the barrel, bolt, breechblock, or any combination thereof.

Collector's FFL - There is no Federal license required to own, possess or collect firearms. However, a Collector's FFL is available to individuals who qualify and wish to apply for one. This license grants the collector expedient ways to acquire certain types of firearms known as "curios and relics" for their personal collection without having to go through a licensed FFL dealer. It grants no special privileges in regards to the acquisition of other types of firearms, and is not a license to engage in the business of dealing in firearms. Federally licensed collectors are required to maintain a record of their firearm acquisitions and dispositions that must be available for inspection by the ATF.

The following is the language from Title 27 CFR Chapter II Sec. 478.125 (f):

(f) Firearms receipt and disposition by licensed collectors. Each licensed collector shall enter into a record each receipt and disposition of firearms curios or relics. The record required by this paragraph shall be maintained in bound form under the format prescribed below. The purchase or other acquisition of a curio or relic shall, except as provided in paragraph (g) of this section, be recorded not later than the close of the next business day following the date of such purchase or other acquisition. The record shall show the date of receipt, the name and address or the name and license number of the person from whom received, the name of the manufacturer and importer (if any), the model, serial number, type, and the caliber or gauge of the firearm curio or relic. The sale or other disposition of a curio or relic shall be recorded by the licensed collector not later than 7 days following the date of such transaction. When such disposition is made to a licensee, the commercial record of the transaction shall be retained, until the transaction is recorded, separate from other commercial documents maintained by the licensee, and be readily available for inspection. The record shall show the date of the sale or other disposition of each firearm curio or relic, the name and address of the person to whom the firearm curio or relic is transferred, or the name and license number of the person to whom transferred if such person is a licensee, and the date of birth of the transferee if other than a licensee. In addition, the licensee shall—

(1) Cause the transferee, if other than a licensee, to be identified in any manner customarily used in commercial transactions (e.g., a driver's license), and note on the record the method used, and

(2) In the case of a transferee who is an alien legally in the United States and who is other than a licensee—

(i) Verify the identity of the transferee by examining an identification document (as defined in § 478.11), and

(ii) Cause the transferee to present documentation establishing that the transferee is a resident of the State (as defined in § 478.11) in which the licensee's business premises is located if the firearm curio or relic is other than a shotgun or rifle, and note on the record the documentation used or is a resident of any State and has resided in such State continuously for at least 90 days prior to the transfer of the firearm if the firearm curio or relic is a shotgun or rifle and shall note on the record the documentation used. Examples of acceptable documentation include utility bills or a lease agreement which show that the transferee has resided in the State continuously for at least 90 days prior to the transfer of the firearm curio or relic.

(3) The format required for the record of receipt and disposition of firearms by collectors is as follows: **(See Table 5)**

TABLE 5: Firearms Collectors Acquisition and Disposition Record

Description of firearm					Receipt		Disposition				
Manufacturer and/or importer	Model	Serial No.	Type	Caliber or gauge	Date	Name and address or name and license No.	Date	Name and address or name and license No.	Date of birth if nonlicensee	Driver's license No. or other identification if nonlicensee	For transfers to aliens, documentation used to establish residency

FEDERAL FIREARMS LAWS AND THE GUN COLLECTOR

Curios and relics (C&Rs) – The definition of C&R firearms appears below. Perhaps the most relied upon portion of this definition is "firearms which were manufactured at least 50 years prior to the current date." If there is a question as to whether any particular firearm qualifies as a C&R, there is a procedure to request a ruling by the ATF. This C&R designation only matters to individuals who have a Collector's FFL. It has no impact on the activity of unlicensed collectors.

> **Curios or relics**. Firearms which are of special interest to collectors by reason of some quality other than is associated with firearms intended for sporting use or as offensive or defensive weapons. To be recognized as curios or relics, firearms must fall within one of the following categories:
>> (a) Firearms which were manufactured at least 50 years prior to the current date, but not including replicas thereof;
>> (b) Firearms which are certified by the curator of a municipal, State, or Federal museum which exhibits firearms to be curios or relics of museum interest; and
>> (c) Any other firearms which derive a substantial part of their monetary value from the fact that they are novel, rare, bizarre, or because of their association with some historical figure, period, or event.
>
> Proof of qualification of a particular firearm under this category may be established by evidence of present value and evidence that like firearms are not available except as collector's items, or that the value of like firearms available in ordinary commercial channels is substantially less.

Class III or NFA Weapons – Machine guns, etc. – Certain specialized firearms are required to be registered with the Federal government and are closely regulated under the National Firearms Act (NFA). They are sometimes referred to "NFA" or "Class III" or "Title II" weapons, and include firearms such as machineguns, short-barreled rifles, short-barreled shotguns, destructive devices (grenades, bombs, etc.), and "any other weapon," a catchall which includes guns such as smooth bore pistols and disguised firearms.

There are many shooters and collectors who enjoy owning NFA firearms in compliance with federal law, but the "how to" is beyond the scope of this work. It is important for gun owners to recognize that possession of such guns without proper previous registration is a felony. Unregistered NFA weapons may range from a submachine gun brought home from WWII by a veteran, to the relatively innocuous smooth bore single shot pistols such as "Handy Guns." At this time, there is no way for a private individual to register an NFA firearm that has not been previously registered.

It is also important to note that terms such as "firearm" and "antique" have a different definition under the NFA than under the GCA.

Federal law on transfer of firearms if you do not have an FFL – Many of the questions on this subject are addressed in the Q&A section of <u>Federal Firearms Regulations Reference Guide</u>. Some excerpts that may be useful appear below. Please refer to the original for the full listing and for citation of the applicable laws. "GCA" refers to the Gun Control Act of 1968, Title 18, United States Code, Chapter 44. "Unlicensed person" refers to an individual who does not have an FFL.

> **Q: To whom may an unlicensed person transfer firearms under the GCA?** - A person may sell a firearm to an unlicensed resident of his State, if he does not know or have reasonable cause to believe the person is prohibited from receiving or possessing firearms under Federal law. A person may loan or rent a firearm to a resident of any State for temporary use for lawful sporting purposes, if he does not know or have reasonable cause to believe the person is prohibited from receiving or possessing firearms under Federal law. A person may sell or transfer a firearm to a licensee in any State. However, a firearm other than a curio or relic may not be transferred interstate to a licensed collector.

FEDERAL FIREARMS LAWS AND THE GUN COLLECTOR

Q: From whom may an unlicensed person acquire a firearm under the GCA? - A person may only acquire a firearm within the person's own State, except that he or she may purchase or otherwise acquire a rifle or shotgun, in person, at a licensee's premises in any State, provided the sale complies with State laws applicable in the State of sale and the State where the purchaser resides. A person may borrow or rent a firearm in any State for temporary use for lawful sporting purposes.

Q: May an unlicensed person obtain a firearm from an out-of-State source if the person arranges to obtain the firearm through a licensed dealer in the purchaser's own State? - A person not licensed under the GCA and not prohibited from acquiring firearms may purchase a firearm from an out-of-State source and obtain the firearm if an arrangement is made with a licensed dealer in the purchaser's State of residence for the purchaser to obtain the firearm from the dealer.

Q: May an unlicensed person obtain ammunition from an out-of-State source? - Yes, provided he or she is not a person prohibited from possessing or receiving ammunition.

Q: Are there certain persons who cannot legally receive or possess firearms and/or ammunition? - Yes, a person who —

1. Has been convicted in any court of a crime punishable by imprisonment for a term exceeding 1 year;
2. Is a fugitive from justice;
3. Is an unlawful user of or addicted to any controlled substance;
4. Has been adjudicated as a mental defective or has been committed to a mental institution;
5. Is an alien illegally or unlawfully in the United States or an alien admitted to the United States under a nonimmigrant visa;
6. Has been discharged from the Armed Forces under dishonorable conditions;
7. Having been a citizen of the United States, has renounced his or her citizenship;
8. Is subject to a court order that restrains the person from harassing, stalking, or threatening an intimate partner or child of such intimate partner; or
9. Has been convicted of a misdemeanor crime of domestic violence
10. Cannot lawfully receive, possess, ship, or transport a firearm.

A person who is under indictment or information for a crime punishable by imprisonment for a term exceeding 1 year cannot lawfully receive a firearm. Such person may continue to lawfully possess firearms obtained prior to the indictment or information.

Q: May a nonlicensee ship a firearm through the U.S. Postal Service? - A nonlicensee may not transfer a firearm to a non-licensed resident of another State. A nonlicensee may mail a shotgun or rifle to a resident of his or her own State or to a licensee in any State. The Postal Service recommends that long guns be sent by registered mail and that no marking of any kind which would indicate the nature of the contents be placed on the outside of any parcel containing firearms. Handguns are not mailable. A common or contract carrier must be used to ship a handgun.

Q: May a nonlicensee ship a firearm by common or contract carrier? - A nonlicensee may ship a firearm by a common or contract carrier to a resident of his or her own State or to a licensee in any State. A common or contract carrier must be used to ship a handgun. In addition, Federal law requires that the carrier be notified that the shipment contains a firearm and prohibits common or contract carriers from requiring or causing any label to be placed on any package indicating that it contains a firearm.

Q: May a nonlicensee ship firearms interstate for his or her use in hunting or other lawful activity? - Yes. A person may ship a firearm to himself or herself in care of another person in the State where he or she intends to hunt or engage in any other lawful activity. The package should be addressed to the owner. Persons other than the owner should not open the package and take possession of the firearm.

FEDERAL FIREARMS LAWS AND THE GUN COLLECTOR

Q: May a person who is relocating out of State move firearms with other household goods? - Yes. A person who lawfully possesses a firearm may transport or ship the firearm interstate when changing his or her State of residence. Certain NFA firearms must have prior approval from the Bureau of ATF before they may be moved interstate. The person must notify the mover that firearms are being transported. He or she should also check State and local laws where relocating to ensure that movement of firearms into the new State does not violate any State law or local ordinance.

Q: What constitutes residency in a State? - The State of residence is the State in which an individual is present; the individual also must have an intention of making a home in that State. A member of the Armed Forces on active duty is a resident of the State in which his or her permanent duty station is located. If a member of the Armed Forces maintains a home in one State and the member's permanent duty station is in a nearby State to which he or she commutes each day, then the member has two States of residence and may purchase a firearm in either the State where the duty station is located or the State where the home is maintained. An alien who is legally in the United States is considered to be a resident of a State only if the alien is residing in that State and has resided in that State continuously for a period of at least 90 days prior to the date of sale of the firearm. See also Item 5, "Sales to Aliens in the United States," in the General Information section of this publication.

Q: May a person (who is not an alien) who resides in one State and owns property in another State purchase a handgun in either State? - If a person maintains a home in 2 States and resides in both States for certain periods of the year, he or she may, during the period of time the person actually resides in a particular State, purchase a handgun in that State. However, simply owning property in another State does not qualify the person to purchase a handgun in that State.

Q: May a parent or guardian purchase firearms or ammunition as a gift for a juvenile (less than 18 years of age)? - Yes. However, possession of handguns by juveniles (less than 18 years of age) is generally unlawful. Juveniles generally may only receive and possess handguns with the written permission of a parent or guardian for limited purposes, e.g., employment, ranching, farming, target practice or hunting.

Q: Are curio or relic firearms exempt from the provisions of the GCA? - No. Curios or relics are still firearms subject to the provisions of the GCA; however, curio or relic firearms may be transferred in interstate commerce to licensed collectors or other licensees.

Q: What record-keeping procedures should be followed when two private individuals want to engage in a firearms transaction? - When a transaction takes place between private (unlicensed) persons who reside in the same State, the Gun Control Act (GCA) does not require any record keeping. A private person may sell a firearm to another private individual in his or her State of residence and, similarly, a private individual may buy a firearm from another private person who resides in the same State. It is not necessary under Federal law for a Federal firearms licensee (FFL) to assist in the sale or transfer when the buyer and seller are "same-State" residents. Of course, the transferor/seller may not knowingly transfer a firearm to someone who falls within any of the categories of prohibited persons contained in the GCA. See 18 U.S.C. §§ 922(g) and (n). However, as stated above, there are no GCA-required records to be completed by either party to the transfer.

There may be State or local laws or regulations that govern this type of transaction. Contact State Police units or the office of your State Attorney General for information on any such requirements.

Please note that if a private person wants to obtain a firearm from a private person who resides in another State, the firearm will have to be shipped to an FFL in the buyer's State. The FFL will be responsible for record keeping. See also Question B3.

NATIONAL FIREARMS MUSEUM STORE

Tel: 703-267-1608   NRAmuseum.com

Get all of your professional firearms and conservation supplies at the National Firearms Museum Store.

We have one of the largest collections of firearms related books and DVDs in the country, with over 600 titles available for sale. (See partial list below.)

We offer all types of gun-cleaning instruction and supplies, featuring the NRA Extreme Performance Gun Kit ® by Mil-Comm Products.

We are a proud distributor and user of Renaissance ® brand wax polish, now available in a 2.25 ounce size as well as the standard 7 ounce size.

We also offer many unique gift items that the gun enthusiast is not likely to find elsewhere.

Some of our most popular books for serious collectors and evaluation purposes:

- *Blue Book of Gun Values* by S.P. Fjestad
- *Flayderman's Guide to Antique American Firearms* by Norm Flayderman
- *Standard Catalog of Firearms*, edited by Jerry Lee
- *Standard Catalog of Military Firearms* by Phillip Peterson
- *Standard Catalog of Smith & Wesson* by Jim Supica & Richard Nahas
- *Book of Colt Firearms* by R. L. Wilson
- *Cartridges of the World* by Frank C. Barnes
- *Pistole Parabellum* (3 volume set) by Joachim Gortz & Geoffrey L. Sturgess
- *The Ultimate Thompson Book* by Tracie L. Hill
- *Mauser Military Rifles of the World* by Robert W. D. Ball
- *United States Martial Flintlocks* by Robert M. Reilly
- *U.S. Military Bolt Action Rifles* by Bruce N. Canfield
- *Complete Guide to the M1 Garand & the M1 Carbine* by Bruce N. Canfield
- *An Illustrated Guide to the '03 Springfield Service Rifle* by Bruce N. Canfield
- *Complete Guide to U.S. Military Combat Shotguns* by Bruce N. Canfield
- *American Engravers, The 21st Century* by C. Roger Bleile

Books featuring the collections at the National Firearms Museum include:

The Illustrated History of Firearms – by Museum Director Jim Supica and Senior Curators Doug Wicklund and Philip Schreier – 304 pages, featuring color photos of 1,500 guns from the Museum, available in hardback, autographed by the authors or in an exclusive paperback edition.

Treasures of the National Firearms Museum – features large-format color photos of engraving masterpieces from the Robert E. Petersen Gallery and historic guns from the NRA collection. Coming in 2013.

Books by Museum Staff: **Handguns** by Jim Supica, **Rifles** by Doug Wicklund & Jim Supica; **Shotguns** by Philip Schreier & Jim Supica. Each presents a brief history of that type of firearm, along with recent photos and catalog listings from modern manufacturers.

YOU, YOUR GUNS, & THE NRA MUSEUM

• **Firearms for Freedom**. Firearms for Freedom is an NRA fund-raising program that seeks the donation of firearms to be auctioned to raise funds for various NRA programs, including the Museum. The Museum reviews all donated Firearms for Freedom guns and can request historic guns or guns of special interest be retained by the Museum for display and educational purposes. Many collectors have seen this as a rewarding way to give back to future generations of gun owners and to step into the ongoing fight to protect the Second Amendment, either as a current gift or as part of their estate planning. Guns donated to The NRA Foundation for educational purposes, such as the Museum, may be tax deductible. For more information contact: 855-4NRA-FFF (855-467-2333).

• **Donations for display.** The Museum is always interested in rare, historic, and important guns for display. The Museum staff are glad to discuss with collectors whether their special guns would be put on display if donated. Occasionally, the Museum will display extraordinary guns on loan. To discuss donation for display, call 703-267-1602.

• **The collectors before you.** Remember, if not for the generosity and foresight of collectors before you, the Museum would not exist. Of the almost 6,000 guns in the Museum system, 99.9% have been donated or are on loan.

The Museum offers a glimpse into the firearms that built our nation, helped forge our freedom, and captured our imagination. The Museum was built by NRA members, and its future depends on NRA members. This is YOUR National Firearms Museum.

NRA
FIREARMS
FOR
FREEDOM

NRAmuseum.com

"Every gun has a story — usually many. Let your treasured firearms inspire the next generation of patriots while preserving our sacred American shooting and hunting heritage."

— *Wayne LaPierre*
NRA Executive Vice President

PROGRAMS OF THE NATIONAL RIFLE ASSOCIATION

COMPETITIVE SHOOTING

Competitions and tournaments: Action Pistol, Air Gun, Collegiate, Disabled, Pistol, Rifle, Silhouette
Postal Matches
National Records
National Rifle & Pistol Championships (Camp Perry)
Bianchi Cup
Muzzle Loading Championships
Air Gun Team Championship & Training Summit
Tournament Operations
Shooter Classification Lookup
Rule Changes
NRA Licensed Target Manufacturers
NRA National Trophies

CLUBS AND ASSOCIATIONS

Club Affiliation
Club Events
Club University
State Associations
Business Alliance

EDDIE EAGLE GUNSAFE® PROGRAM

Grants for schools, law enforcement agencies, daycare centers, hospitals, and libraries
Mascot Costume Contest for law enforcement agencies
School Programs

LAW ENFORCEMENT ACTIVITIES

Police Pistol Combat Competitions
Tactical Police Competitions
National Police Shooting Competitions
Tuition-Free Armorer Schools
Law Enforcement Instructor Development Schools
Officer of the Year

FIREARM EDUCATION

Basic Firearm Training Program
Gun Safety Rules
Short-Term Gunsmithing Schools
Winchester/NRA Marksmanship Qualification Program
Shooting Sports Camps
Basics of Personal Protection In The Home DVD
Basics of Personal Protection Outside The Home DVD
Fundamentals of Gun Safety VHS

NRA Basic Courses include:

Pistol
Rifle
Shotgun
Home Firearm Safety
Personal Protection in the Home
Personal Protection Outside the Home
Muzzle Loading Rifle
Muzzle Loading Pistol
Muzzle Loading Shotgun
Metallic Cartridge Reloading
Shotgun Shell Reloading
Range Safety Officer

GUN COLLECTING

Gun Shows

HUNTER SERVICES

Environment, Conversation, and Hunting Outreach Program
Great American Hunters Tour
Hunters for the Hungry
Hunters' Rights
Hunter Clinic Instructors
Youth Hunter Education Challenge
Youth Hunter Education Challenge DVD

PROGRAMS OF THE NATIONAL RIFLE ASSOCIATION

INSTRUCTOR, TRAINING COUNSELOR, AND COACH TRAINING

American Sport Education Program
Instructor Certification
Coach Education & Development
Training Counselors

NATIONAL FIREARMS MUSEUM

Exhibits
Firearm Conservation
Museum Library

RANGES

Online Registry of Places to Shoot
Range Development & Operations Conferences
Range Grants
Range Technical Team

REFUSE TO BE A VICTIM®
PERSONAL SAFETY PROGRAM

Seminars
Certified Instructors

WOMEN'S PROGRAMS

Women's Awards: Sybil Ludington Women's Freedom Award
and Marion P. Hammer Woman of Distinction Award
Women's hunts (Women on Target® Hunting Programs)
Firearm education for women
(Women on Target® Instructional Shooting Clinics)
Women's Wildlife Management/Conservation Scholarship
Women's Wilderness Escape

YOUTH PROGRAMS

National Junior Shooting Camps
Outstanding Achievement Youth Award
Youth Education Summit (Y.E.S.)
Youth Education Summit DVD
NRA Shooting Sports Camps
Youth Wildlife Art Contest

NRA'S HEADQUARTERS RANGE

Matches
Training

FRIENDS OF NRA

Banquets & Autcions

NRA.ORG
NRAMUSEUM.COM

Preserve the Right to Keep and Bear Arms for this and future generations — JOIN THE NRA

The Institute for Legislative Action (ILA) is the lobbying arm of the NRA. Established in 1975, ILA is committed to preserving the right of all law-abiding individuals to purchase, possess and use firearms for legitimate purposes as guaranteed by the Second Amendment to the U.S. Constitution. ILA's ability to fight successfully for the rights of America's law-abiding gun owners directly reflects the support of NRA's nearly 4 million members—a number that has more than tripled since 1978. When restrictive "gun control" legislation is proposed at the local, state or federal level, NRA members and supporters are alerted and respond with individual letters, faxes, e-mails and calls to their elected representatives to make their views known.

In 1986, the NRA and millions of gun owners nationwide applauded as the Firearms Owners' Protection Act was signed into law by President Ronald Reagan. ILA worked for more than a decade to secure passage of that historic legislation to reform the Gun Control Act of 1968.

Combined with the strong grassroots efforts of NRA members and NRA-affiliated state associations and local gun clubs, the Institute has worked vigorously to pass pro-gun reform legislation at the state level.

These efforts include enacting laws that recognize the right of honest citizens to carry firearms for self-protection; preemption bills to prevent attacks on gun owner rights by local anti-gun politicians, and fighting for legislation to prevent the bankrupting of America's firearms industry through reckless lawsuits.

The Institute is also involved in educating the public about the facts concerning the many facets of firearms ownership in America. Through the distribution of millions of printed fact sheets, brochures and articles annually and the posting information and the latest news daily on its Internet site (www.nraila.org), the Institute provides facts about responsible firearms ownership, the Second Amendment and other topics.

In NRA Headquarters in Fairfax, Va., and in offices in Washington, D.C., and in Sacramento, Calif., the Institute employs a staff of more than 80, with a team of full-time lobbyists defending Second Amendment issues on Capitol Hill, in state legislatures and in local government bodies.

While NRA is a single-issue organization, the Institute is involved in any issue that directly or indirectly affects firearms ownership and use. These involve such topics as hunting and access to hunting lands, wilderness and wildlife conservation, civilian marksmanship training and ranges for public use, law enforcement-related issues, product liability, trapping, crime victim rights and criminal justice reform.

The NRA Institute for Legislative Action

NRA-ILA

We the People

Protecting our Second Amendment Freedom and Hunting Heritage

WWW.NRAILA.ORG

NRA NATIONAL FIREARMS MUSEUM

2014

16-MONTH CALENDAR
INCLUDING SEPTEMBER THROUGH DECEMBER 2013

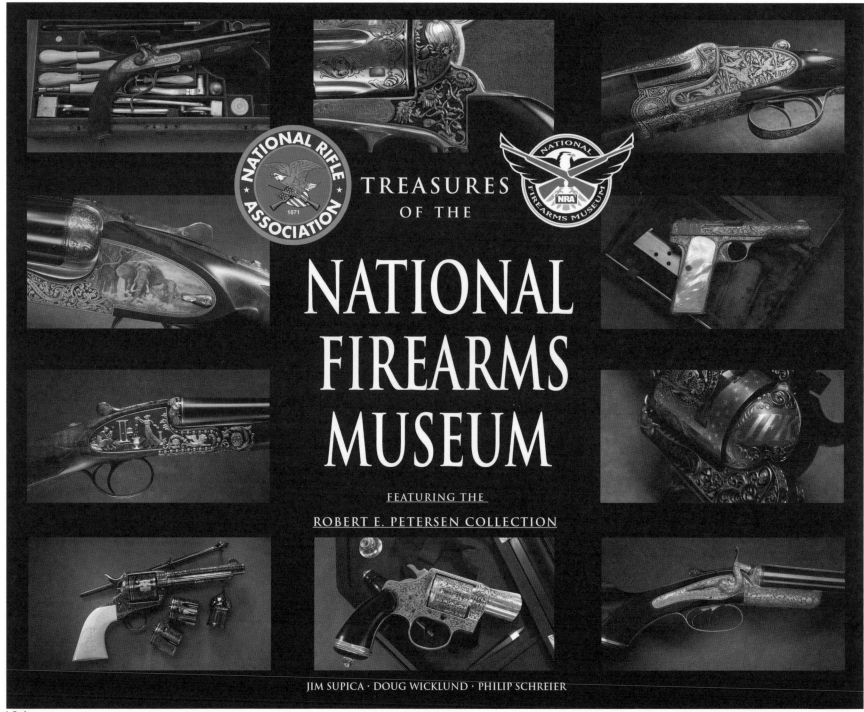

TREASURES OF THE

NATIONAL FIREARMS MUSEUM

FEATURING THE

ROBERT E. PETERSEN COLLECTION

JIM SUPICA · DOUG WICKLUND · PHILIP SCHREIER